The Bible Study Leader's Handbook:

Getting Started

By Brent Mackey

Published by Brent Mackey
117 Lansmere Way
Rochester NY 14624

Edited and Designed by Amber Linson.

ISBN: 979-8-9866684-0-6

Printed in the U.S.A.

First Edition

Table of Contents

Acknowledgment

Bob Stuhlmiller – my friend and Bible researcher. He helped me find the answers and I miss him, but we'll be together again.

Don Fay – Thanks for letting me pick your brain. You were a wonderful mentor and supporter.

Chris Bacus – Your insights and guidance were invaluable. Thank you for all the opportunities to serve.

To my students that over the years were always with me in Bible studies- Tim Wallace, Ron Krolak, Jack Burnette, Johnny Rowe, Ken Harrington, John Gage, Mike Rivoli, Diane Crevelling, Carol Bocanelli, and Gary Mastrella. I could always rely on you.

Mike and Diane Gmitter – thanks for being my sounding board and for all the great advice.

Bobbie Mackey – my beautiful understanding wife – I couldn't have had all the Bible studies without her encouragement.

Preface

When I was young, my mother was the superintendent of a Presbyterian church. Therefore, I grew up hearing the stories of the Old Testament. I believed in God, but this belief was born by my parents telling me that there was a God, not by a building of faith through interest or understanding.

As I grew up and time went by, the morals of the country changed and so did the rules and beliefs of many churches. My inherited faith became confused as the country moved through free love, new age, ESP, Witchcraft and even new findings in science. Many other alternative faiths, all claiming to be true, came into being or became more pronounced. Let the force be with you, the Baha'i faith, Moonies, psychics and many more. I still believed what I was told, that there is a God, but I continued to struggle with my murky faith. Therefore, I looked into many of those alternative faiths, but was never satisfied in what I found.

When I finally got back to the Christianity, vowing to give it one more try, I was resolved to find out what the Bible was all about. At that time in my life, I didn't want to get involved with organized religion. There was too much dissention among the different church denominations. I wanted to read the Bible and look at different commentaries to try to understand, or discard, the Christian faith.

I studied and studied, watching TV preachers and considering their take on the Bible. Things were confusing. It seemed that these teachers didn't want to give me the secrets of how to understand the Bible. They talked in circles and gave their own opinions without giving the real kernels of truth needed to make logical sense out of the pages of God's Word. Even after studying, it still seemed confusing.

Finally, I decided to do my own Bible Studies. Every morning I would read from a set of books called Thru the Bible by J. Vernon McGee. I enjoyed his homespun humor and the way, as he put it, "The cookies are put on the bottom shelf so the kids could get them." It was his way of saying that he made it very understandable for all seekers to start learning about the Bible.

It was a wonderful experience and for 1 year and 3 months, I enjoyed every page in his entire set of books. What started out to be a very daunting task, turned into a real love as every day I would sit longer and longer reading God's word and McGee's short commentary after each section. This study made me realize how wonderful the Bible truly is.

While I was reading Thru the Bible, I met a friend (Bob) one day for lunch. We had never talked about God before (although we'd known each other for over fifteen years). For some reason I started to tell him about these wonderful books I was reading. A strange look came over his face and he said, "You won't believe this but I was trying to read the Bible over the weekend. I have tried and tried to read the Bible and as usual, this last weekend was no different - I just could not understand what the Bible was talking about. I threw the Bible across the room and said 'God if you want me to understand your book you've got to send me someone or something.'" After our discussion, Bob started reading Thru the Bible with me. He caught up to me and finished before I did.

It turns out, I needed someone to help me as a study partner and Bob needed help finding a way to connect with the Bible. I of course didn't know that at the time, but God did. The ground was as fertile as it could possibly be for us to get together to study God's word and encourage each other. Through this and many other instances, I've come to understand that God is involved with our everyday lives, to help us not to hurt us. He will bring just the right people together to teach, encourage and help at the exact time it's needed. What an Awesome God!

So, after about 3 months of reading McGee's books, Bob and I started discussing what we were reading. We would often sit up half the night mulling over Bible principles and checking other commentaries on the Bible. We always ended up reading the real authority, the Bible. Then, we would determine which commentator we felt had the right perspective on a particular point or on some non-essential theory we wanted to nail down. In our study we used to say "The Bible Reads," it meant that whatever the Bible says is the correct answer and is the only answer we use. That was the single most important rule we adopted. Although to some this may seem boring – but I can tell you, it was the most rewarding experience I have ever had.

Some theologians try to stretch or twist the scriptures and others leave things out. After going over all the sources we had, it was apparent that even the best theologians, who obviously love Jesus with all their being, can be biased and twist scripture to make an illogical point. We found that their desire to twist Scripture was usually because it affected a bigger point that they or whoever taught them were trying to prove. Perhaps a pet theory of their own or the idea of the denomination they represented. They didn't want a particular scripture to hamper the larger idea they believed to be very important.

The final authority and the one that should always be above all other books is the Bible. Therefore, when you come to a Bible study leave preconceived ideas and things you have been taught back at home. Read what the Bible actually says. Be flexible enough to look at each verse with new eyes and an open mind to understand the truth contained in God's Word.

I asked a retired preacher if I could go to lunch with him every week. I would buy him lunch and in return he would let me pick his brain about the Bible and any other topic that I felt was relevant to the study of the Bible. It later became a three-person Bible study as Bob joined us.

We met at a restaurant and our studies were so full of controversy and energy that people actually told us that they came to the restaurant to hear us discuss the Bible. I soon learned that discussing things when people have opposing views could really enhance a Bible study. The one big rule is that we respect one another's right to disagree. That may seem easy but it took a while and a very patient preacher/teacher who met with us every week to show us by his attitude what it means to be humble and love each other. His name is Don Fay – you may have seen some articles and short stories by him in different publications. He was instrumental in helping me to grow as a Christian and a Bible study leader.

My first "open" Bible study was for men only. It was at my home and it continued for over 10 years. There was no restriction as far as church affiliation or denomination. The dynamics changed every week, as different people would come. Our maximum amount that came was 15 men. Our year-end parties drew all the people that came at different times throughout the year. A truly diverse group and a great learning experience.

The pattern of Bible study for the men's group was the idea of sharing views. If any opposing views were present everyone started looking up Scriptures to see who they felt was right about a particular point. It was fun to see these men sitting around a table all scrambling through the Bible to read the next passage of scripture that might shed more light on the discussion. Even though we may end the night with no clear point won, we all learned and had a great time. It's about reasoning together and coming closer to the truth when we do. Certainly, this can only be done if the leader has established the idea that Christians can agree to disagree on non-essential points. The essential points of Christianity have to be rock solid and are certainly expressed that way in the Bible.

The next Bible study we had was mainly for women. It was at Bob's house and it was designed to include Bob's daughters and friends. This Bible study lasted over 7 years. It gave me a good opportunity to understand the dynamics of a Bible study for woman. It was different from the men's group and I had to learn the best way to introduce the Bible for the best understanding possible for each group.

The more I was exposed to different groups of people, the more I was able to adapt and change my approach in keeping with the group dynamic.

My goal was and is always: give the students what they need to learn the Bible in the most understandable and memorable way.

When I started understanding the Bible and its correlations, it became very easy to figure things out for myself. After understanding the keys to unlocking God's truth, I really was upset with all the teachers and preachers who wanted to keep that knowledge to themselves.

I had found a church that I felt was good, and Don Fay, who had retired from that church, after meeting with me over a period of months thought that giving Bible studies would be a good fit for me. He of course was right. The excitement of watching others find out what I had found out was thrilling to say the least.

Over the course of the next 25 years or so, I was privileged to give thousands of Bible studies. God has blessed me in a spectacular way. Previously, I had trained many people in other areas of my work life. Now I was able to talk about what became my hearts focus and has stayed that way to this day, Jesus and God's Holy Word.

I had a leg up on giving Bible studies because of my previous training experience. However, I still wanted to learn about the specifics of a Bible study. I found there wasn't anything written about it. I bought several books that sounded like exactly what I wanted only to be disappointed. Therefore, in giving Bible studies I had to learn how to do it the most effective way by experience.

Years later, I got it into my head (hopefully God given idea) that it would be a boost if anyone wanting to give a Bible study could read something that gives the ABCs of Bible studies. I've seen a tremendous amount of studies start and then very quickly die out. This book is for the person that wants to give Bible Studies.

Since 1995, I've given weekly Bible studies, sometimes giving as many as seven different Bible studies per week extending over several years. These Bible studies have lasted from 4-6 weeks (a special study for witnessing to non-Christians) to over ten years with the same group of people.

At the time of this writing, I am currently giving three Bible studies during the week and teaching an adult class at my church on Sunday. Over the years, many people have given their life to Christ from these Bible studies. I consider it a privilege and an awesome responsibility that the Lord has allowed me, by His grace, to be involved with so many people studying His word.

-Brent Mackey

Introduction

This book is best suited to help people that have at least a working knowledge of the Bible and the desire to give effective Bible studies. Throughout this volume, you will discover tips and organizational ideas that will enable you to determine the type of Bible study that is needed for a particular group. It will also show the way the Bible study should be given for optimum effectiveness as well as specific purposes that help Christians grow in their walk with the Lord.

This volume will also show you what you need in terms of skill sets to add to your own personality. So that you can take what you already have in your own arsenal and add just the right amount of new ideas and techniques to really hone in and capitalize on what God has already given you.

Beginning with the key elements necessary to start a good Bible study, I will go over the spiritual parts as well as the physical parts necessary to be successful.

This book will also give you insights on eliminating studies that are boring. It's not hard if you understand the steps you can take to make people feel comfortable, and fill their spiritual needs. People who come to Bible studies want to be a part of a knowledgeable group of Christians and have their preconceived ideas met.

You will understand how a step-by-step approach to teaching the Bible can involve and invigorate people in their walk with Christ.

You will also learn about easy and interesting ways to help you understand the principles of walking with God in your life. Using Christ as an example, you will learn how to take the applications of life principles and make them simple, logical and easy to follow for the people attending your class. Tips and ideas will make people have that "illumination" that encourages everyone to come back to your class for more.

The idea of making people steadfast in the love of Jesus is often a tough job. The world doesn't help train many Christian morals today. You will learn how to bridge the gap through education, truth and knowledge. You will be able to understand how to educate people in a way that will ring true and people will remember.

People need to learn about how a Christian can make an 18" trip from the head to their heart to love God and have a greater faith. You will learn that your show of compassion, caring and love for them will affect them in a way that will change them in their own walk with the Lord.

Everyone comes to situations with their own expectations. We all do. You will see how understanding and knowing what those expectations are can be crucial to your success. We cannot think that everyone is normal the way we are normal. We have to realize how important the differences are and how we can satisfy expectations even if they differ from our own. You will see a step-by-step method of finding and fulfilling these expectations.

You will also find tips, hints and ways to actually get a Bible study started. This is probably the hardest part of a Bible study for most people. If you know the secrets, then it's just a matter of putting one foot in front of the other and getting it done. It's not hard at all. You just have to know the best way you feel works for you and is the most comfortable way to approach the task.

There is a method of teaching that is the most productive and by far the most interesting to students. In this book, you will learn what that method is and how to follow through with it in your classes. It's the easiest method and the one that will be the best way for you to teach and keep people coming back to your class for more. The people will also retain more and be hands on with their own learning. Once you understand and try it, you will never want to go back to the older ways of teaching the Bible.

You will also add to your arsenal four actual Bible studies that have proven to be eye opening and get the people excited about learning more in the Bible. I've included them to help you understand concepts as well as give you Bible studies you can do for anyone. They are stand-alone Bible studies in that, you do not have to use them over a long period of time. In one of these studies, you can show the awesomeness of God and give good application principles. It's all in "stand alone" 1 night lessons.

The Bible is the greatest book ever written. It was inspired by God and has no equal in any other book in the world. This is provable by a preponderance of the evidence. If people understand that, then faith is cemented in their hearts. We have a Savior but as the Ethiopian asked Philip in Acts 8:31 after Philip asked him if he understood what he was reading in the scriptures – he said, "how can I unless someone explains it to me."

People need someone. There are people that only you will be able to get through to. People need you to help them. I wrote this book to help you get it done.

Chapter I

"Always be prepared to give an answer to everyone who asks you to give the reason for the hope you have."
(1st Peter 3:15)

Getting Started

The first time I realized how important Bible studies were, I was in a customer's home to talk about remodeling their kitchen. We had exhausted questions about the project when they asked me to stay and have a cup of coffee with them before leaving.

Besides being busy with my business, I had started reading the Bible and the books surrounding what the Bible was saying in light of the culture in which it was written. The insight I was getting from my reading was so exciting that I couldn't help sharing it with this couple.

You know how much you want to tell someone something that you just found out or learned. That's how I was. It was as if I had to share it because the knowledge was too great not to. That was me. I was studying the book of Ruth at the time. It's a love story but so much more. I asked them if they would like to learn something about the Bible that I thought was really good. They said sure. I asked them if they had a Bible I could borrow to show them what I was talking about. They did.

They were not practicing Christian people, but I saw their eyes widen as I told them about the correlation of the different customs and what it meant. I could see that this was the first time anyone talked with them about what is actually in the Bible.

I never knew whether they went to church or investigated anything after I left. They decided not to do anything with their kitchen, so I never saw them again. However, I can tell you what they said to me that day that has inspired me ever since. They said, "You make the Bible come alive". What a great feeling to have someone say that. I wasn't trying to do anything but explain what I'd been reading. I have come to understand I was giving a Bible study.

I didn't know anything about a Bible study and had no actual desire to become involved in giving Bible studies at that point in my life. However, I'll never forget the compliment that has spurred me on to this day: "You made the Bible come alive!"

-Brent Mackey

Bible studies are so important to Christians today. With the world changing so fast and our lives seemingly out of control there is only one place we can go to have real peace. That is to the Word of God. A Bible study can be conducted by anyone with a minimum amount of knowledge, a love for the Lord, and the desire to teach. Through this chapter, we will discuss the necessities of a successful study and how you can get things started with your own group.

A Bible study is a unique environment for meetings because any number of combinations and people can make up a study. It could be a single person (same gender), all males, all females, mixed group, different backgrounds, young, old, or both. The dynamics and requirements may change, but when it is done well faith is built and Biblical knowledge is increased.

The atmosphere in smaller groups lends itself to asking questions and involving the students as you are making the relevant points during the lesson. The questioning enables the teacher to bring out ideas to be highlighted by the answers that people are giving. As the amount of people attending grows, studying would lend itself to more of a seminar, lecture type of Bible study. This is a necessary approach for a larger church Bible study. However, for the smaller group setting, questioning during the lesson engages your students and energizes them in a very special, rewarding way.

There are hidden benefits to the questioning style of teaching in smaller groups. One of which is you as the teacher will be able to understand what people are thinking as they answer the questions. This is immensely helpful as incorrect ideas are often brought within their responses. Another helpful by product is often the question asked brings about a broader discussion than anticipated. That is because one of the answers given crosses over to a topic that is somewhat related. Great discussions often occur that add to the excitement of the study.

As far as the group's gender make up is concerned, we cannot overlook that fact that differences may exist. It's been my experience that generally men and women are different in their interests when studying the Bible. Knowing this is possible, depending on the subject, it's important to be sensitive to either group. Ensure that everyone is getting the questions and information they need to understand the points being made in the study.

You may have noticed that when it is a single person, I put same gender. This is important, because the situation can be misconstrued and the Bible study tainted if two people from the opposite sex have a private Bible Study. I know that today this practice is acceptable. However, a Bible study should be beyond any kind of reproach. At times, people seem to enjoy casting doubts on the intentions of Christians (even other Christians). It's better to err on the side of being too cautious than not cautious enough.

Every person who follows Christ is a disciple. However, to help you accommodate the types of dynamics, establish a general system for people in the Bible study group. Use the acronym BODY, as in the body of Christ, to understand the needs and expectations for each people group.

- B= Baby - New Christian
- O= Older brother- is one that goes to church and some knowledge of the Bible
- D= Disciple of Christ- been walking with the Lord and going to Bible Studies for a little while but not long – has a working knowledge of the Bible
- Y= Years of Discipleship – long time involvement with Bible studies

Using this method to create questions will ensure that you include all people and give every group questions appropriate to their experience.

Which Bible

Regardless of the group makeup, we need to be ready to meet people in a way that makes them comfortable. In order to teach people from different religious backgrounds, I carry a four-part parallel Bible. This book includes The King James Version, The Amplified Version, The New American Standard Version and the New International Version (1984). This Bible shows all four versions in four columns over both pages. Two columns each page, each column with a different translation. They are extremely helpful in any teaching situation. I can read from the Bible our group has agreed to use and if new people have a question concerning a different translation they have been using, we can look at theirs as well as the other two in order to get a consensus of the thought and meaning in that area of study.

It is also helpful to have those different translations for the overall atmosphere of the group. Instead of being dogmatic about teaching, the fact that we consult different translations is interpreted to be "fact finding learning" as opposed to forcing one's opinion on others. The study takes on a free and open feeling where everything is open for discussion.

The two translations I lean on most are The King James Version (KJV) and The New International version (NIV). The King James Version (KJV) is most widely recognized by people that I meet. Not to have it as a comparison could be an obstacle to witnessing, because of a person's Biblical bias. It is however, a harder Bible to understand because of the way it's written. By contrast, The New International Version (NIV) is more easily read and understood, especially for beginners. Nevertheless, the perception of some is that the "real" Bible is KJV. Therefore, having both Bibles included in one book solves this dilemma.

The other two versions help with any clarification and often give a broader understanding. By comparing different translations, we are able to see different words used for the same meaning. In so doing we get a richer, deeper overall meaning.

Bible publishers themselves are forced to change wording. This is because in order to have different translations, Bible publishers have to change a minimum amount of words in the texts without losing the original context and understanding. They do this to avoid accusations of plagiarism that could arise from using identical phrasing. However, we as Bible students and teachers get the benefits that come from it.

Many other Bibles are great resources for study. However, for the sake of this book, I will be putting both The King James Version (KJV) and The New International Version (NIV) together in the smaller sections quoted from Scripture. In the larger sections, I will use the NIV. I find that it is much less confusing for beginning students. Whichever version you use, remember, Bible study builds faith as long as people can understand what they're reading.

> **"Consequently, faith comes from hearing the message, and the message is heard through the word of Christ."**
> **(NIV Romans 10:17)**

> **"So then faith cometh by hearing, and hearing by the word of God."**
> **(KJV Romans 10:17)**

I have discovered, over the years, that there are different Bible studies needed for different people groups, as well as different topics and styles depending on individual levels of maturity. This book is especially designed with the smaller Bible study groups in mind (usually less than 30 people). Witnessing and helping Christians to mature in Christ should be centered on God's word whenever possible. Do not forget, "The Bible Reads."

Chapter II

"you also, like living stones, are being built into a
spiritual house to be a holy priesthood, offering
spiritual sacrifices acceptable to God through Jesus
Christ."
(NIV 1st Peter 2:5)

Key Elements to a Bible Study

My livelihood has always been in remodeling and construction work. As such, building becomes an easy way to explain how and why things go together. If I were to pick four essential ingredients to building they would have to be the architect, the blueprint (and material), the foreman and workers, and the method of communication in order to ensure a good lasting structure is built.

The Architect needs know exactly what is to be built. He then must get his points of design and proper building practices across to the foreman and inspectors. It will need to be flawless under scrutiny by experts. Every code and requirement must be met. The foreman can go to the Architect for clarification on any point, should he need more knowledge about his plan. He will have taken everything needed into consideration for the structure to hold up and pass the test of time.

The blueprints are the way that the architect shows his design work. They must be legible and easy to understand. The plans must be simple enough to explain to a customer yet complex enough to give all the information needed to the foreman. They also must be written to include everything in the clearest most concise form for the inspectors. That necessitates an economy of words and symbols so every piece of information can be seen when looking at a single page. This ensures no misunderstandings or contradicting information that would confuse the building process.

The Foreman has to implement the architect's plans properly in the right order and with a respect for the Architects knowledge and eye for design. During planning, the foreman must organize and coordinate the construction process from start to finish. He must be able to communicate the information to his workers, as well as the customers, so each knows what to expect. He must instill confidence from both workers and customers by studying and educating himself in all the different aspects of the projects.

The method of relaying information to the parties involved must be organized and consistent. It also must be flexible in regard to whom the information will be imparted. For example, the Building Inspector requires a product sheet detailing all the information concerning materials used, the workers need installation preparation information, and the customer will focus on pricing, appearance, reliability, and performance. Special attention must also be given to checks and balances that guarantee the information is received properly.

When everything works together the harmony of the different parts can bring about the desired effect and result. All parties are satisfied with the aspects of the project and can have a certain pride about not only finishing what they set out to do, but also getting it accomplished the right way. The same rings true for Bible studies. The understanding of these construction elements is very similar to the elements that make up a study.

-Brent Mackey

Key Elements

Now that we have introduced some concepts and ideas about giving Bible studies in chapter I, the next step is getting prepared to share the Gospel message.

The four main essentials for a Bible study are The Holy Spirit, The Bible, the leader, and the method of teaching. This mixture of elements reminds me of the building process. God tells us in the Bible that we can think of Him as a builder, although His building is spiritual.

For example, in the Old Testament Abraham was looking for the Promised Land, the writer of Hebrews in the New Testament draws a parallel of that incident.[1]

> **"For he was looking forward to the city with foundations, whose architect and builder is God." (NIV Heb 11:10)**
>
> **"For he looked for a city which hath foundations, whose builder and maker is God." (KJV Heb: 11:10)**

The Holy Spirit

God is like the Architect in building a structure. He is the creator and has thought of every contingency possible. He has a master plan for His

---

[1] Commentary on Hebrews 11:10 by Adam Clarke
Whose builder and maker is God - The word τεχνιτης (Greek) signifies an architect, one who plans, calculates, and constructs a building. The word δημιουργος (Greek) signifies the governor of a people; one who forms them by institutions and laws; the framer of a political constitution. God is here represented the Maker or Father of all the heavenly inhabitants, and the planner of their citizenship in that heavenly country. See Macknight.

creation. In addition, He has given spiritual guidance by sending the Holy Spirit to guide us in our quest to know Him better. Jesus said:

He will bring glory to me by taking from what is mine and making it known to you.

> **"And we also thank God continually because, when you received the word of God, which you heard from us, you accepted it not as the word of men, but as it actually is, the word of God, which is at work in you who believe."**
> **(NIV 1Th 2:13)**

> **"For this cause also thank we God without ceasing, because, when ye received the word of God which ye heard of us, ye received it not as the word of men, but as it is in truth, the word of God, which effectually worketh also in you that believe."**
> **(KJV 1Th 2:13)**

The Bible is our essential object of study. It is the only way we can truly learn about God.

The Study Leader

The Bible study leaders are like the foreman on the construction project. By Anticipating questions that will be asked and using the Bible and guidance of God, rightly divining the correct answers becomes easier and easier. They study the Bible themselves to understand different points and ideas expressed in the Bible. Using extra information if needed to understand details and correlations will enable the leader to gain the knowledge to confidently teach whatever lesson is desired. An essential for people desiring to do this type of work is to have a love for God's word.

In the Bible, we find this verse:

> **"Do your best to present yourself to God as one approved, a workman who does not need to be ashamed and who correctly handles the word of truth."**
> **(NIV 2nd Tim 2:15)**

"Study to show thyself approved unto God, a workman that needeth not to be ashamed, rightly dividing the word of truth."
(KJV 2nd Tim 2:15)

Being a Bible study teacher is one of the most honorable aspirations imaginable. It is a wonderful position to be able to watch people grow in faith before your eyes. There is, however, a responsibility on the part of the teacher to do all they can to prepare and be prepared to lead it. It's a thrilling time and a great chance that God has given you.

The Method of Teaching

A total teaching plan includes a good method to explain God's message to the people. It should be given in the most understandable way possible taking into consideration the group of people receiving it. Too often, the right message is given in a way that makes understanding it a hard task. In Corinthians, Paul notes an effective way of communicating the Gospel message to the people:

> **"To the weak I became weak, to win the weak. I have become all things to all men so that by all possible means I might save some."**
> **(NIV 1st Cor. 9:22)**

> **"To the weak became I as weak, that I might gain the weak: I am made all things to all men, that I might by all means save some."**
> **(KJV 1st Cor. 9:22)**

In our method, we must always consider who we are talking to and how we can best approach them. That means we have to consider how they need the message delivered, not necessarily how we want to deliver it.

All of the preceding ingredients are important to having a great Bible study. Missing any one of them will mean we will miss the opportunity God has given us to get His message out. There is so much more information on these subjects that can make a good Bible study really "Rock". In the next four chapters, I will be expanding on each one of these important elements.

Chapter III

"because our gospel came to you not simply with words, but also with power, with the Holy Spirit and with deep conviction. You know how we lived among you for your sake."
(NIV 1st Th 1:5)

Key Elements: The Holy Spirit

A young woman, about 25 years old, was in a Bible study I was teaching. She had been in the group for 4 months or so when I noticed she was becoming more inquisitive. Her excitement built as we were studying about Abraham and Isaac. She noticed similarities between Christ and Isaac when Abraham was to sacrifice Isaac on the mountain. All of a sudden, she blurted out "Do you mean that there really is a God?" It was phrased as a question and spoken as a statement.

Her face beamed and her eyes told the whole story. Wide with wonder and full of energy she was letting me know that the Holy Spirit had just given her the gift. She put it all together and it was now real to her. What a wonderful night.

I have been truly blessed by God to see several people have the same look come over them. There is not a look on someone's face that can be better than when a person realizes, deep in his or her heart, that there is a God, His word is true, and His Son is our Savior. The Holy Spirit gives that gift. We cannot see Him, but we certainly can see the result of His influence on our lives. I only hope you can have the same experience. Thank you, God!

-Brent Mackey

Defining the Holy Spirit

The Holy Spirit is the third part of the trinity or "Godhead" (As the totality of God is called in Acts 17:29, Romans 1:20 and Colossians 2:9 KJV).

Within the trinity, there are three parts: Father, Son and Holy Spirit. The order is so named because that is how God wants us to think of Him. It is also in the chronological order of procession, which means it is in the order of a specific presence as stated in the Bible. First "God created the heavens and the earth"; we would attribute that to God the Father being the creator. In addition, the majority of the Old Testament attributes the interaction with man to God the Father. The Son is presented in prophecy in the Old Testament but in actual presence as a baby in The New Testament. He grew up and told us, after He goes to the Father, the Holy Spirit would come. The Holy Spirit is third in procession.

Nevertheless, God is One. When we look in the Bible at all 66 books, we find many things are attributed to all three. There is no distinction between them in terms of being God. However, this is a hard concept to understand, especially to beginners.

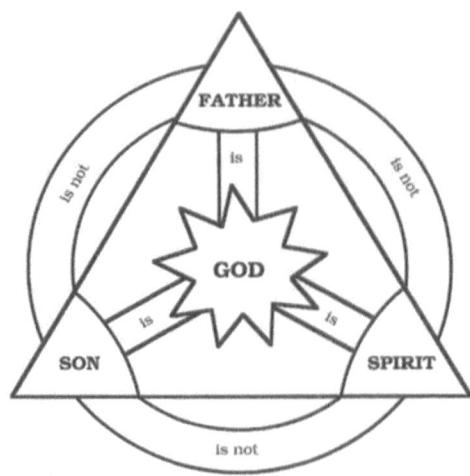

Figure 1. Diagram from: Emberson, Iain A. "The Trinity." Christianity in View: The Trinity, 22 Feb. 2016, christianityinview.com/trinity.html.

This symbol, and many more like it, started being used in the early Church to denote the Godhead or the Holy trinity. Sometimes called personages of the Trinity, you can see the parts are distinctly separate. However, God flows through all of them and wants us to understand them as being One. This was how the early church helped people to understand this relationship between the elements of the Trinity. When we read in the Bible the phrase "in the name of the Father, Son and Holy Spirit" (Matthew 28:19) and yet it talks of God as one, it's a hard concept to grasp. You see that even in that phrase it is not names of but rather name singular. The symbol helps to understand the concept but it remains clear as mud.

Attempts to explain the trinity have come in many other ways. The most often heard likeness is that of the three states of H20: Water, solid, and vapor. All the same make up, but in different states.

This led me to another idea regarding the elements of a computer that helped me personally understand the relationship. A computer is made up of three basic parts. They are the hard drive, monitor and mouse/keyboard. Even though you can buy each piece individually, it is not a computer until you put all three together. This seemed logical, however nowhere near the true complexity of the God of creation.

Similar to the computer, we cannot separate the Father, Son and Holy Spirit. Throughout the Bible, God makes it clear the Trinity is to be thought of as one. As it is with the computer. If you separate any part of the computer, it ceases to be a computer. It then becomes parts, but of no value at all as a computer. This is a crude example of the trinity because God is so much more, but it helped me to understand the three in one concept.

The Holy Spirit's Illumination

The Holy Spirit's role in Bible study cannot be overemphasized. Without His illumination there would be no possible way people would be able to understand the vast complexities of God throughout the Bible. We know the role of the Holy Spirit because, like many things, it is defined for us within the pages of the Bible.

> **"But the Counselor, the Holy Spirit, whom the Father will send in my name, will teach you all things and will remind you of everything I have said to you."**
> **(NIV John 14:26)**

> **"But the Comforter, which is the Holy Ghost, whom the Father will send in my name, he shall teach you all things, and bring all things to your remembrance, whatsoever I have said unto you."**
> **(KJV John 14:26)**

It is not necessary for the Holy Spirit to teach us all the information in all the libraries in the world. That is not what is being said here. The Holy Spirit teaches us all the things that God wants us to know. At the time He wants us to know it. Everyone is different and God gives each of us the knowledge we need to have. It may be different from one person to another, never contradictory. You will hear people say "I can't believe it; I've read this same verse a hundred times and just now saw something different in it. That is a God thing. He will help us recall things of importance. This is not an immediate infusion of knowledge; it happens over time. As you read the Bible, things just automatically start being clear and simple.

We learn about God and Christ from the Bible, but the Holy Spirit helps us to understand, correlate, and apply the things He teaches us. He validates things about Christ and God's word. He also helps us with the discernment God wants us to use. God, however, does not do our work for us.

Have you ever heard the slogan "Let go – Let God"? To some this phrase indicates that the believer should get out of the way and God will handle everything. It pre-supposes the idea that God wants to handle all our problems and wants total control over our lives absent of our inept intervention. This concept is not accurate.

If God wants to control us and do everything for us, why would He want to teach us anything? Maybe He just wants to have us be His robots? Is that the answer for the above slogan? The Bible tells us that the opposite is true.

> **"8 This is to my Father's glory, that you bear much fruit, showing yourselves to be my disciples.
> 9 As the Father has loved me, so have I loved you. Now remain in my love."
> (NIV John 15:8, 9)**

> **John 15:8 "Herein is my Father glorified, that ye bear much fruit; so shall ye be my disciples.
> John 15:9 As the Father hath loved me, so have I loved you: continue ye in my love."
> (KJV John 15:8, 9)**

The Holy Spirit Works in Us

The Holy Spirit is to act in accordance, and consort with the Bible in helping the believer's search for the things of the Lord in all avenues of learning. Everyday life and experiences become even better as we can see God's plan unfold before our eyes. He helps all of us as students and teachers to understand Bible verses and the truth about Jesus. He acts inside the Bible, prompting us to greater and greater heights of Biblical knowledge. Through His power, we persevere in our study of God's word.

Can the Holy Spirit teach us all of what the Bible means by supernatural power? The answer is yes, He can; God can do anything. However, it seems that God wants us to learn by searching, listening, asking questions, and talking with others about His word.

"Consequently, faith comes from hearing the
message, and the message is heard through the word
about Christ."
(NIV Romans 10:17)

"So then faith cometh by hearing, and hearing by the
Word of God."
(KJV Roman 10:17)

"Then Philip ran up to the chariot and heard the
man reading Isaiah the prophet. "Do you understand
what you are reading?" Philip asked.
"How can I," he said, "unless someone explains it to
me?" So he invited Philip to come up and sit with
him"
(NIV Acts 8:30, 31)

"And Philip ran thither to him, and heard him read
the prophet Esaias, and said, Understandest thou
what thou readest?
And he said, how can I, except some man should
guide me? And he desired Philip that he would come
up and sit with him."
(KJV Acts 8:30, 31)

The Holy Spirit takes that learning and makes it real to us. It's the Holy
Spirit who puts things in the proper perspective for us and fits the pieces
together.

Teachers versus the Holy Spirit

Is there any scriptural basis for teachers even though the Holy Spirit is here
to teach us? Absolutely there is:

"Now an angel of the Lord said to Philip, "Go south
to the road--the desert road--that goes down from
Jerusalem to Gaza." So he started out, and on his
way he met an Ethiopian eunuch, an important
official in charge of all the treasury of Candace,
queen of the Ethiopians. This man had gone to
Jerusalem to worship, and on his way home was
sitting in his chariot reading the book of Isaiah the

prophet. The Spirit told Philip, "Go to that chariot
and stay near it."
Then Philip ran up to the chariot and heard the man
reading Isaiah the prophet. "Do you understand
what you are reading?" Philip asked.
"How can I," he said, "unless someone explains it
to me?" So, he invited Philip to come up and sit with
him."
(NIV Acts 8:26-31)

In the above case, the Ethiopian eunuch was reading and trying to understand the Bible. His choice of words when asked if he understood what he was reading was "How can I, unless someone explains it to me."

Now, we know that the Holy Spirit was sent to help people understand about the Lord. In the Ethiopian eunuch's answer, we see the idea that God also chose people to help spread the word and explain Scripture. Maybe it is because humans learn so much from the Bible when someone like himself or herself helps to correlate different Scriptures and teaches them. At the same time, we know that the Holy Spirit will help people understand this instruction. The Bible specifically tells us that some are given to be teachers.

"And in the church God has appointed first of all
apostles, second prophets, third teachers, then
workers of miracles, also those having gifts of
healing, those able to help others, those with gifts of
administration, and those speaking in different kinds
of tongues."
(NIV 1 Cor 12:28)

"And God hath set some in the church, first apostles,
secondarily prophets, thirdly teachers, after that
miracles, then gifts of healings, helps, governments,
diversities of tongues."
(KJV 1 Cor 12:28)

In addition, James admonishes us that not all should aspire to be teachers because if we become teachers we will be held to a different accountability. Why again do we need teachers if the Holy Spirit will do it all?

"Not many of you should presume to be teachers,
my brothers, because you know that we who teach
will be judged more strictly."
(NIV James 3:1)

"My brethren, be not many masters, knowing that
we shall receive the greater condemnation."
(KJV James 3:1)

As for teaching those that are already Christians, there are many areas in the Bible that address that, but the scripture that says we are to teach Christians is in Matthew. It is part of the great commission.

"Therefore go and make disciples of all nations,
baptizing them in the name of the Father and of the
Son and of the Holy Spirit, and teaching them to
obey everything I have commanded you. And surely
I am with you always, to the very end of the age."
(NIV Matt 28:19, 20)

"Go ye therefore, and teach all nations, baptizing
them in the name of the Father, and of the Son, and
of the Holy Ghost: Teaching them to observe all
things whatsoever I have commanded you: and, lo, I
am with you always, even unto the end of the world.
Amen."
(KJV Matt 28:19, 20)

Teaching in the church is so important that the Lord, himself, gave us instructions as a command to do exactly that. If Jesus wanted the Holy Spirit to teach us everything, he wouldn't have commanded us to teach.

Holy Spirit versus Other Spirits

"Dear friends, do not believe every spirit, but test the
spirits to see whether they are from God, because
many false prophets have gone out into the world."
(NIV 1John 4:1)

"Beloved, believe not every spirit, but try the spirits whether they are of God: because many false prophets are gone out into the world."
(KJV 1John 4:1)

From the preceding verse, we know there are many spirits that may want to trick us into believing something untrue. Therefore, we are to test the spirits. It would be absurd to test the spirits by the spirits themselves. John is saying that feelings alone or ideas that pop into our heads may not be good. We need to check these things out with the Bible. The Word of God will help us discern a false prophet or spirit.

It therefore becomes essential for students to check out the Scriptures and try to objectively understand the meaning that is being conveyed. If it is not in agreement with what we feel it should be, we need to put feelings and emotion aside and let the "Word of God" take priority. We then, must change our thinking about the subject in question to be aligned with God's word, not the other way around.

Some years ago, there was a preacher in Florida that was supposed to be able to impart the Holy Spirit to people. Some churches were planning trips down to see him and learn what special gift this preacher had and how they could get the power from him. As I talked with a friend who was buying into this man's stories, I asked him to check out some web sites and see what the man stood for. He checked him out and found that the fruits did not measure up to his claims.

He acted so ridiculously that he bragged about healing a man by punching him in the face. Obviously, this was absurd. Also, no real miracles that could be proved were found. The more ridiculous his claims, the more obvious it became that the fruits of his ministry were false. My friend concluded that this preacher was a false prophet. He arrived at that conclusion by seeing that this preacher/healer was not acting the way the Bible tells us men of God act. Thank God He has given us His book to be able to test people who make false claims about spiritual gifts and/or the Holy Spirit.

The Holy Spirit Is a Necessity

Considering the Biblical foundation concerning teachers, we should obviously be learning from them. However, we are to remember good teaching and the Holy Spirit work together. Every Bible study needs the Holy Spirit to be a part of it.

"**As for you, the anointing you received from him remains in you, and you do not need anyone to teach you. But, as his anointing teaches you about all things and as that anointing is real, not counterfeit-- just as it has taught you, remain in him.**"
(NIV 1 John 2:27)

"**But the anointing which ye have received of him abideth in you, and ye need not that any man teach you: but as the same anointing teacheth you of all things, and is truth, and is no lie, and even as it hath taught you, ye shall abide in him.**"
(KJV 1 John 2:27)

When a person comes to the Lord, the Holy Spirit testifies that Jesus is God in the flesh. The feelings, concerning who Jesus is and was, will become stronger. The truth becomes discernable and the Holy Spirit builds our faith as we read God's word. Teachers are needed but only the Holy Spirit is able to testify with our Spirit that the things of Christ are true and accurate as is stated in the Bible. Those kinds of feelings cannot be made real to us except by the Holy Spirit.

That teaching by the Holy Spirit is what some people call the "18- inch difference."18 inches is the approximate distance between our head and our heart. The Holy Spirit teaches our heart (Inner being) that what God says, and the facts surrounding Jesus life death and resurrection, are true. They become part of our deep belief about God and His promises.

The Holy Spirit's Fruit

As well as teaching us about the truth of Christ, the Holy Spirit also conveys the conviction, sin, and judgment to the world. This aspect of the Holy Spirit is the reason why some people come to the Bible study in the beginning. He teaches in a way that no one else can teach by making him or her feel the need for Jesus. He also plows the ground and softens people's hearts so they will listen to good Bible teaching. Therefore, it is so important to have us realize the Holy Spirit's part in Bible studies.

"**But the fruit of the Spirit is love, joy, peace, patience, kindness, goodness, faithfulness, gentleness and self-control. Against such things there is no law.**"
(NIV Gal 5:22-23)

**"But the fruit of the Spirit is love, joy, peace,
longsuffering, gentleness, goodness, faith,
Meekness, temperance: against such there is no
law."
(KJV Gal 5:22-23)**

We also know that it is possible for the Holy Spirit to bring just the right someone into people's lives to help them learn. God is so wonderful and compassionate. I believe that when we go to meet the Lord, we will find out that He was in our lives much more than we could ever imagine.

So, what does the fruit of the Spirit have to do with Bible study? A teacher who exhibits these gifts will find students more receptive and willing to learn. By seeing a teacher modeling Christ, the students will see the better way and start practicing the fruits of the Spirit very quickly. This idea will be covered in a later chapter. However, let me just say that letting students take the lead in a Bible study, listening to the people in the group, and dealing with pre conceived false ideas, will be so much easier and effective if we utilize the gifts of the Spirit as we address these issues in Christian love.

Chapter IV

"Therefore, having this ministry by the mercy of God, we do not lose heart. But, we have renounced disgraceful, underhanded ways. We refuse to practice cunning or to tamper with God's word, but by the open statement of the truth we would commend ourselves to everyone's conscience in the sight of God."
(NIV 2Co 4:1, 2)

Key Elements: The Bible

Being older has many advantages to my Christian walk. The one thing that is most prominent is that my memory starts with a time in this country when everyone went to church. In my elementary school we were divided by whether we were Protestant or Catholic. This was not a division between groups as no one really cared about which church our friends belonged to. It just meant that some of us went for religious education at a Catholic church and the others went to the Protestant church. We all had the same Bible and an extreme reverence about religion.

Unlike today Christ teachings permeated our lives. All of the television shows talked about the Christian religion from time to time. Early movies had parts of it that concerned our Christian faith. In John Wayne's movie "The Searchers" Ward Bond played a Reverend. After crossing a river with Indians chasing them he hands a wounded man a Bible and tells him to hold it and it will make him feel good. On the "Rifleman" the second episode Lucas tells Mark about the story of Job in the Bible. "Wagon Train," "Leave it to Beaver," "The Andy Griffith Show" all affirmed the belief in God. Every show and movie in that era reinforced Christian principles and ideals.

Later as I grew older the church I attended disappointed me in the way they were allowing their own ideas to pervert the Bible. I left organized religion and didn't look at it again until I was 42 years old. But, I am certain that my upbringing helped me recognize I needed to reexamine my values and listen to the Holy Spirit's convictions. The disillusion I felt in my youth made me concerned about how to deal with the Word of God. It made me investigate the Bible more closely without trying to learn about it from only one source.

That is why teaching the Bible is so important. People need to know that there is a faithful and true place to go to that will help them understand life's important questions.

A place where knowing God and the truth will ease their concerns and cares and give a purpose to life.

-Brent Mackey

What is the Bible?

The Bible is the Word of God and it contains within the pages an insight and knowledge that transcends human understanding. The more the Bible is studied the more complex and wondrous it becomes. It is both a window to our purpose, and a way to understand God. Our understanding will be with the degree of illumination that God allows to come to those who diligently study its meanings and precepts.

Mainly, the Bible is the object of our studies.[2] Sometimes a Bible study will deviate from the literal study of the Word of God. This can be done to define a cultural period spoken of in the verses being discussed or for a matter of clarification on a situation that requires historical knowledge to understand the points being made in the study. This should be done infrequently and purposefully. The reason is because the Bible defines itself as the Word of God and we are told to meditate on God's word. As such, the object of our attention and study should always be focused on The Bible.

We are also told in the Bible that:

> **"All Scripture is God-breathed and is useful for teaching, rebuking, correcting and training in righteousness, so that the servant of God may be thoroughly equipped for every good work."**
> **(NIV 2Tim 3:16, 17)**

> **"All scripture is given by inspiration of God, and is profitable for doctrine, for reproof, for correction, for instruction in righteousness:**
> **That the man of God may be perfect, thoroughly furnished unto all good works."**
> **(KJV 2Tim 3:16, 17)**

---

[2] A.W. Tozer, a respected 20th century theologian said:
"For a child of God, the Bible is the book of all books, to be reverenced, loved, pored over endlessly, and feasted upon as living bread and manna for the soul. It is the first best book, the only indispensable book. To ignore it or neglect it is to doom our minds to error and our hearts to starvation".
(The Alliance Weekly/Witness, 1950)

The Origin of the Bible

The Bible was written over approximately 2000 years by 40 plus authors who were inspired by God to write down the words contained in it. The oldest book in the Bible is Job and the date of its writing is uncertain. We know it predates the first five books written by Moses at approximately 1450-1500 BC. They were the next oldest books written after the book of Job. The last books written were the New Testament penned by different authors between 40 and 95 AD. As the books do not carry any copyright dates scholars are uncertain of the exact dates.

The writings of the Bible are dated by the way words are used in the text, the way letters are written and the writing style used in the manuscripts. The writings are also verified by the historical references concerning events surrounding the time of the writing and the events spoken of that were prior to the writing. Also, omitted events help scholars to determine the age by realizing some events hadn't happened yet, at the time of the writing.

As a person studies the Bible, it becomes obvious that no mere mortal or group of mortals could ever have written such perfect literature. The prophecy and foreknowledge contained within the various books, chapters, and verses are certainly surprising to new students and will be instrumental in building understanding and faith. This is the benefit of reading the Bible and seeking God within its pages. Obtaining deeper faith, more understanding, and a confidence in our Christian conduct should be our goal. Through a better understanding and deeper faith, we also will have a more certain hope in the future that can never be understood by secular men and women. Most importantly, it brings a deeper belief in Christ and His gift on the cross.

Different Bible Versions

As the Bible is such a pivotal aspect of understanding God, we must choose the right "version" to use for the group we will be teaching. The term "version" refers to the exact Bible that has been published. Each Bible covers the same material. However, it is important to know how different Bibles have been translated. This will then give you a way to determine what particular group the Bible is intended for. We also have to be wary of certain types of Bibles that have a low level of scholarship.

There are tremendous amounts of Bible versions to choose from. I shy away from making absolute statements about any one version. The important things to look for in a Bible are who was involved with the version, and how was it translated.

First, only consider Bibles that are translated inter-denominationally. In other words, translators from all different types of churches should be involved with the translation. Baptists, Presbyterians, a Lutherans, and others - even atheists are all right to help. This is as long as their prevailing goal is to give the best translation of the Greek, Hebrew, and Aramaic words into the language of the people. In this way, the biases of the individual denominations will be nullified. Some versions boast of having over 70 translators from 20 different denominations. Credentials are important, but with large numbers of translators from different groups present, good scholarship is insured. One translator cannot include his own preconceived ideas or bias into his translation. This is because all words and meanings implied by the translation have to be proven to and approved by the rest of the group. Once proven accurate, they can be included in the final work. Checks and balances are so important.

As for the types of Bibles available, let me first go over three types of translations and then another consideration:

- Word for word translation (Also called literal). In this version, the translators use the best single word wherever possible for the Greek, Hebrew or Aramaic word used in the early manuscripts. Using this style of translating will make a version harder to understand as in some places extra words, which we might use in the normal writing of today, are not used. (Examples of this type of translation are: The King James Version (KJV), and the New American Standard Bible(NASB).

- Thought for thought translation (Also called Dynamic equivalent). This version is translated to give a person the sense of the same thought being conveyed but with the phrasing, figures of speech and grammar we use today. This implies in some cases a degree of knowledge of what was being meant by the author; translators have to use their best guess in situations where the meaning could be taken in two or more different ways. The dynamic equivalent uses some license in translating, but it is still using the same structure and wording, as much as possible, to the earliest manuscripts. (Examples of this type of translation are The New International Version (NIV), and the New Revised Standard Version (NRSV)

- Paraphrased Version (Also called Free Will). This version seeks to translate the meaning of the text in the most understandable way using language of today. The phrasing and wording are left up to the translators without trying to adhere to the original structure. This means more flexibility in translation to maintain the priority of readability. This type of version is easiest to read but gives the translators more latitude and creases the opportunity for opinion to creep into the actual meaning of the text. (Examples of this type of translation are the Good News Bible (GNB), and the Message (MSG)

All versions using multiple translators strive to deliver a Bible as close to the original meaning as possible.

Selecting the Right Bible

The next issue is what group of people will be using this translation. Children have different Bibles than adults and it would depend upon the age group to determine the appropriate Bible. Likewise, there are different Bibles for different education levels. Usually beginners would use Bibles that have less formal wording. For people just starting out it has been suggested to use Bibles translated to a 6th grade education level. That may sound like it is overly simplified, but it is not. Beginners like it because the overall understanding is easier. As far as Bible studies are concerned, there is no problem in using a NIV, or New King James, or others that read at a 6th grade level, because those Bibles meet everyone's needs.

As we go up the level of understanding and critical details mean more, the word usage changes somewhat. It becomes a translation that doesn't flow as easily. This is because of a desire to use more accurate wording without adding anything extra. The actual words used are also more specific although they may not be widely known.

As part of the preparation for a study, a teacher should consult a stricter version like The King James Version or The New American Standard Version for clearer more concise understanding of the passages to be studied.

A Matter of Opinion

Why are there so many different Bibles? This question comes up often. Certainly, education level and usage is one reason. However, there is also another reason, copyright laws. The Bible is and has always been the most popular book ever printed. Bible sales far exceed any other book sales worldwide. The first book commissioned to be printed on a printing press by our government was the Bible. Because of copyright laws, in order for a publisher to be able to publish a Bible it would have to be substantially different from one that has a copyright already.

In order for a publisher to capitalize on the demand for Bibles, a new one with different words would have to be translated. It would have to be a Bible that carries the same message that doesn't change any meaning, but uses some different words throughout. In our country, it means all kinds of Bibles for all kinds of usages. Adhering to the copyright laws, publishers need to change the proper number of words per line or volume in order to legally publish a new Bible. We are blessed to have so many choices from which to pick. That enables us to have just the right Bible for the purpose we need.

In conclusion, as long as the criteria stated earlier is met, to assure unbiased translations with good scholarship, it is a personal choice on which Bible to use. In terms of the Bible study, it would be good for the leader to establish a Bible to suggest for a student who does not have one. He or she must select a Bible with the degree of difficulty appropriate for the students attending. There are guides to show the level of each version to better help you establish the correct one for your class. Check where you buy your Bibles for help. However, if a student has a different Bible they want to use, there is no problem having them use their own for the class.

Chapter V

"Anyone who breaks one of the least of these commandments and teaches others to do the same will be called least in the kingdom of heaven, but whoever practices and teaches these commands will be called great in the kingdom of heaven."
(NIV Matt. 5:19)

Key Elements: Leadership

During the last 25 years, I have attended several Bible studies conducted by different teachers. Aside from ministers and pastors, the leaders were generally well-meaning people trying to help others understand the Bible. Some were particularly interested in teaching the things that moved them the most.

Many of those started out great, but ended rather quickly. The reason most leaders gave for stopping was a lack of interest by the people attending.

Some people are natural leaders, but no matter how much raw talent exists, they still need to learn how to apply it in their field of endeavor. Leading Bible studies is no different. Molding a person's gift includes learning how and why people enjoy coming to a Bible study. It is not about doing it the way that the leader deems proper. It is about fulfilling the desires of the people coming. That changes to a lesser or greater degree with the start of every new class.

-Brent Mackey

Defining a Facilitator

The leader of a Bible study is generally a person who can help people understand principles and concepts contained in the Bible. Also, wherever possible, they allow the awesomeness of God to be seen through the pages of the Bible. The best way I have found to do this is by being a Facilitator.

So, what is a facilitator? It is a person who, after reading Bible verses and introducing Bible ideas, asks questions about what has been said. By asking questions and guiding the conversation, the leader will generate a wonderful learning experience. This is accomplished because the facilitator teaches by encouraging conversation within the group. He in effect is encouraging people to take an active role in the study. Even if people do not actually want to talk, they will still be thinking of how they would have answered the questions.

How and why

Because the leader is taking a journey with the students, a small group setting makes it easiest to be a facilitator. If he brings the students along with thoughtful questions, they will enjoy the trip much more. These guiding questions are the key to facilitating. The group has the opportunity to show the leader not only where they are in their understanding, but also where they want to go next. Although some answers may have to be solidly defined for learning to take place, everyone is thinking about what is being said.

Oddly enough, the mind works better if it is preparing to use the mouth to speak. If people know they might be speaking soon, they will listen more in preparation to speak. When you are planning to say something and you engage your mind before talking, you will organize your thoughts better and the words will come out the way you want them to. It is in thinking about talking that the person will learn and remember far more readily than just listening to a speaker.

What is the Difference?

Too often Bible study leaders simply read the Bible, and fill up their time speaking about what was read. They will read articles about the passage, pass around maps while telling the people what the maps show, open up a book about culture and read a section to help understand the historical effect, and then give a short sermon on what the Bible verses mean. The Bible study ends without ever engaging the people that have attended it. There is not enough time allowed for any discussions at all. After working so hard to prepare a great study, and giving a large amount of information, unfortunately the attendees may not have been engaged throughout the entire study.

That is why being a facilitator, and using questions to guide and engage, has worked best for me. I can assess the amount of interest, or even boredom, in the group. It is better to find a good subject about the Bible passage to talk about rather than to drone on trying to give them all of the information you prepared. If people are bored, they will not want to spend their time coming back.

Example Question

Let me give you a quick example of how facilitating works:

In reading Genesis 1:1, what does "In the beginning God created the Heavens and earth" mean? What would your answer be? Write your answer on the lines below:

_____

_____

_____

_____

The question is written in a way that engages your mind to work on the question before I give you the point I hope to make.

The mind is an enormously wonderful thing that God created. It seeks to answer questions correctly. So, whenever a leader asks a question, everyone in the class would want to have the right answer. It is human nature to want to be the first to get the answer right. Just like everyone would desire to serve that tennis ace, hit a home run, or excel in anything else that they may be doing. In the Bible study everyone would like to stand out in class as being able to get it right, occasionally.

The Answer

So, what about the answer? What did you guess the correct answer was? Did you exhaust all possible answers to the question, even if it is only in your mind?

I could have asked, "What does it mean 'in the beginning'?" However, to unlock your mind to be ready to accept the answer and remember it, I find that people need to concentrate on trying to think of what the answer could be. By exhausting all possible answers, the human mind is yearning to resolve the question to its conclusion. When the answer is finally given even if it only validates your correct answer, you will remember the whole subject discussed better. If I had asked a more pointed question, the people listening would not have been as engaged in trying to guess what I wanted for an answer. So, they meditated on God's word a little longer and when we talk about the answer everyone will put the information in the right part of their brain. Because the area that holds all the information about the subject has been activated.

As a side light, the answer that I am looking for is: it means the beginning of time as we know it. This concept is so hard for us to wrap our minds around. But, God lives in a place called eternity. It is a place where time has no beginning or end. He then created a place where time was finite. Our world came into being. Therefore, it had to have a beginning and God's Word also tells us there will be an end. Genesis tells us when and how time began. Science tries hard to go through theories that tell us what the scientists think happened. However, the Bible gives us who, what, when, and where it all took place. What a wonderful God we have, He knew we would want to know this information.

Example- Teaching the Awesomeness of God

Along with facilitating, a good leader will show the awesomeness of God whenever possible. Here is just one example of how that is done.

If a study included Moses bringing down the tablets containing the Ten Commandments, then here is what we would read in one portion of the scripture:

> **"When Moses approached the camp and saw the calf and the dancing, his anger burned and he threw the tablets out of his hands, breaking them to pieces at the foot of the mountain. And he took the calf they had made and burned it in the fire; then he ground it to powder, scattered it on the water and made the Israelites drink it.**
> **He said to Aaron, "What did these people do to you, that you led them into such great sin?"**
> **"Do not be angry, my lord," Aaron answered. "You know how prone these people are to evil. They said to me, 'Make us gods who will go before us. As for this fellow Moses who brought us up out of Egypt, we don't know what has happened to him.' So I told them, 'Whoever has any gold jewelry, take it off.' Then they gave me the gold, and I threw it into the fire, and out came this calf!"**
> **Moses saw that the people were running wild and that Aaron had let them get out of control and so become a laughingstock to their enemies. So he stood at the entrance to the camp and said, "Whoever is for the LORD, come to me." And all the Levites rallied to him.**
> **Then he said to them, "This is what the LORD, the God of Israel, says: 'each man strap a sword to his**

side. Go back and forth through the camp from one end to the other, each killing his brother and friend and neighbor.'" [28] The Levites did as Moses commanded, and that day about three thousand of the people died."
(NIV Exodus 32:19-28)

There is a tremendous amount of material to talk about in these verses. The leader could talk about Moses' righteous anger, about Aaron lying (because he had someone make the golden calf) and what people do without God in their lives. He could also talk about taking the right side and punishment. Contained in the history of the event are so many ideas that are helpful to understanding life's principles. We certainly can see why God wanted us to know what happened to the people at that point in time.

What about understanding the awesomeness of God? Do we see anything in these verses that could bring us back to the message of salvation? (If so, this may be why God included some of the information in the verses to begin with)

The last phrase says that three thousand people died when the Law came down the mountain with Moses. The people already knew that they should be worshipping God, but they chose to make a graven image instead. They knew their actions were wrong.

So, three thousand people died after God gave them the Law. They already knew they were sinning. Moses brought down the Law showing them in writing that they were sinners and they still refused to repent.

But there is also something here that can help us understand, or help establish the awesomeness of God and His foreknowledge. It will also point to Christ and His gift of life through His sacrifice on the cross. So, let us look at a few verses in the New Testament. We can use the actual words of the Bible to give us some insight on how the Bible, being one whole book written by over 40 authors over 1600+ years, has certain cohesiveness with repetitive meaningful ideas.

First a foundational verse:

"For God so loved the world that he gave his one and only Son, that whoever believes in him shall not perish but have eternal life."
(NIV John 3:16)

> **"For God so loved the world, that he gave his only begotten Son, that whosoever believeth in him should not perish, but have everlasting life."**
> **(KJV John 3:16)**

So now, let us look at another time in history. A time when the church was formed based on the saving grace of Christ. At this time history went a little differently. The people believed in Jesus and wanted to know what they should do to take the next step in coming to the Lord.

> **"Therefore let all Israel be assured of this: God has made this Jesus, whom you crucified, both Lord and Christ."**
> **When the people heard this, they were cut to the heart and said to Peter and the other apostles, "Brothers, what shall we do?"**
> **Peter replied, "Repent and be baptized, every one of you, in the name of Jesus Christ for the forgiveness of your sins. And you will receive the gift of the Holy Spirit. The promise is for you and your children and for all who are far off--for all whom the Lord our God will call."**
> **With many other words he warned them; and he pleaded with them, "Save yourselves from this corrupt generation." Those who accepted his message were baptized, and about three thousand were added to their number that day."**
> **(NIV Acts 2:36-41)**

How many were added to their number when the church was formed? Three thousand! Three thousand died when the Law was given and three thousand were saved on the day the church began – on Pentecost when the people were baptized and received the gift of the Holy Spirit.

We can never make doctrine on anything in the Old Testament but we can see the light of the New Testament reveal a truth in the Old Testament that helps to show us a bigger principle contained in the New Testament.

> **"The Lord is not slow in keeping his promise, as some understand slowness. He is patient with you, not wanting anyone to perish, but everyone to come to repentance."**
> **(NIV 2 Peter 3:9)**

"The Lord is not slack concerning his promise, as some men count slackness; but is longsuffering to us-ward, not willing that any should perish, but that all should come to repentance."
(KJV 2 Peter 3:9)

We can see now why God may have chosen to give us an exact number in the Old Testament. God could have had the authors write down that "many" were slain on that day. But, God chose to have the exact number be used in the Old Testament. He also chose the exact same number to be used in the New Testament writing.

So, what can we say then that this number helps us understand? It is like underlining the ideas of the New Testament: Christ died for everyone and therefore is able to save everyone that comes to Him, and God does not want anyone to perish.

Only God could ever arrange the numbers to work out exactly like it did. Only God could have known 1500 years before Pentecost that the exact number who died when the Law was given would be important to know.

It is also important to answer the question of coincidence. Maybe it was just a coincidence that the numbers were the same. That is a possibility, however God inspired the Bible to be written, He is the one who inspired these numbers to be written down. In my opinion He wanted us to know that the Law could not bring salvation, people died upon its coming. But, Jesus brought salvation up close and personal on the day that the church was formed. On that day, 3,000 people were baptized into eternal life. So then, 3,000 people died when the Law was given and 3,000 people were saved when they came to Christ on Pentecost.

Making connections like these with your students will reinforce the awesomeness of God, and these connections can be found throughout the Bible and should be used wherever possible. As a facilitator, mixing these connections with guiding questions will do a great deal in keeping the students engaged. This engagement then opens the door for the Holy Spirit.

The Idea of Coincidence

Having given my opinion, I will not deny the idea of coincidences. I know that at some point in these Bible studies students will want to talk about that possibility. It is logical to conclude that sometimes it may be just be coincidence. We cannot prove either way. Events could be just similar. So, we should always speak from the side of truth and strength in our studies. Allowing it is "possible," only adds credibility to our teaching.

But there will come a point when all these coincidences mount up; prophecies will have been proven to be true and the foreknowledge of God has been seen. The awesome truth of Christ and God's word is revealed to them, and then the students will realize it could only come together because of God's involvement. That being the case, then God inspired the entire Bible. It is the Bible itself that will build people's faith and trust in God if we just study it.

Handling Questions

It is the leader's job to study the Bible ideas and verses before the actual Bible study time. This will enable him/her to answer questions that come up.

There is much more we can talk about and do talk about in a Bible study. However, by giving people a question and opening the floor for anyone to talk, everyone learns. That is a facilitator. This is someone who enjoys the conversational way of learning.

So often people will have a quizzical expression on their face and start to ask a question, only to find as they are talking that they have answered their own question. To a facilitator, it does not matter who is talking, providing people are learning the correct things. And when someone finds their own answer, because of this process, they will never forget it.

Putting It All Together

So, a leader (facilitator) becomes an integral part of the Bible study process. They ask the right questions to stimulate the student's ability to find the right answers. A leader does this by searching out verses and ideas in the Bible.

The Holy Spirit makes the Bible real to your student's spirit; it resonates as true and wonderful in the deepest core of their being. As you watch people grow in the Lord and realize that you are a part of that growth you will come to understand the role that a Bible study teacher has in the lives of their students. This will spur you on to greater and better ways of teaching.

Chapter VI

"We are therefore Christ's ambassadors, as though
God were making his appeal through us. We implore
you on Christ's behalf: Be reconciled to God."
(NIV 2 Co 5:20)

Key Element: Method of Teaching

I discovered after years of teaching that people learn on their own terms. However, there is an order of learning that seems to work best, and it transcends all groups. First, people learn how to do something. Then they get good at it. Next, they start learning why they do what they do in the way they do it. That seems to be the best way to learn. I have never been as successful using any other order of procedure.

I have also discovered a learning curve that applies to most learning experiences. Of course, there are always exceptions, so this is a generality. It takes approximately one year to become proficient at doing anything. After that year most people look like they know what they are doing and can do some aspects skillfully. During the next three years, they really get a grip on it and excel to the point of being considered a professional. After this period, things start making sense and people start to understand the how and why.

The same thing applies to Bible study students. I've found the first thing a student wants to learn is general navigation of the Bible itself. It will seem a complex and difficult thing and will take time before a general overall knowledge of where to find things is accomplished. The second thing that occupies their interest is the life of Christ in the Gospel messages. The third thing is the Bible stories of Genesis and Exodus fascinates them. After that, people start being excited about the Bible in general, as by this time they have an excellent basic knowledge to build on. Then students start wanting certain books of the Bible studied as well as areas of study like end time prophecy.

Knowing these steps, it is important to develop an organized format that fulfills the learning desires of everyone attending. It should also help teachers to understand that it takes time to get proficient at knowing things in the Bible. Everyone in a Bible study is on his or her own time schedule and each person is in a different place in the learning cycle.

-Brent Mackey

Teaching and Appealing

The goal of leading a Bible study is to teach people the love God has for them and the fulfillment of that love in Christ. Then reinforcing that idea, Bible studies will also teach how we should consider others and in what ways we can glorify God in our own actions every day of our lives. Keeping their attention during the study itself is therefore important to ensure the duration of the study achieves the before mentioned goals. To that end, the method of teaching must both maintain the student's desire to be in the class while at the same time enabling them to understand and remember what the Bible is saying. To achieve this combination, it is a good idea to understand what draws people to a Bible study.

The Method

As defined in the previous chapter, my preferred leadership style is facilitating. The method around this style is questions and discussions. By using personal connections, material questions, and open discussions the facilitator is able to create an environment that is comfortable for the attendees while opening the door for the Holy Spirit to join the group.

As students become more comfortable, they also become more active. Things become clearer when everyone has the chance to ask questions until their curiosity is satisfied or their confusion is cleared up. Through the conversations the students feel a sense of belonging and value as a member of the group. Coupled with that is the expectation of having a good experience and learning something at the same time. So, not only will they enjoy attending, but they will also begin each meeting with a willing mind.

The facilitator of a Bible study is taking the class on a journey of learning by exploration and discovery. Most attendees will learn something that excites them and makes them yearn to tell their friends that they learned some great things in their class. That applies to everyone from beginner on up.

Preparing to Teach

When you teach you are performing. Your job is to convey information in a way to make it understandable and memorable. That takes delivery preparation. When I first learned to talk with people, I learned a script word for word. It took 3 days of memorization to get it down. Then it took another month of saying it to people until I knew it well enough to use it as if I were talking normally with expression.

Now, I want to say something that might sound contradictory. Learning something to that extent is a freeing situation. The reason is that when you know exactly what you are going to say, even if you take a slight diversion now and then, you can still cover points fluidly. If something is said that must be responded to before you go on, it never bothers you because you know where you are and where you want to go. You become free to watch people's reactions and adjust your conversation and expression to be able to get your ideas across to others in a better way.

Preparation Guidelines

Minimum requirements needed to ensure a good learning experience:

- Good preparation to enable the leader to answer most basic questions about the verses studied
- Question sheets for the students
- Teacher sheet with answers for the leader (Also side notes to start conversations)
- Current events or everyday things to mention that parallel some of the lessons in the verses

If you want to come off more professional rehearse your class. If you are planning on reading the verses take some time to pre-read the sections. This way you will not stumble over words. Look up difficult words to ensure that you know the correct meaning. If you are making any correlations to other scriptures make sure you have them written down and write notes that remind you of other things to make the study smoother. A small amount of preparation will give everyone in the class a feeling of confidence in you as their teacher.

Teachers Preparation Sheet

A teacher's preparation sheet is a good way to help you organize your thoughts and be prepared for you class. Your style and preferences will help you to decide for yourself what you want to keep, discard, or add. To help get you started I have included a basic layout for a preparation sheet which you can find at the end of this chapter.

As you will notice, the sheet is most helpful when it follows the flow of the class and takes into account as many discussion points as you can think of that will come up during the study. Therefore, not only do we include verses and the potential commentary to accompany them, but also prayer requests and current events. When encompassing the whole study in this way we make it easy to remember what was discussed in previous meetings, and maintain a sense of organization and professionalism.

This sheet is for your notes, but it can also be used to help you when you are making your student sheets of questions. The idea then, is to ask questions that will lead to the understanding of the points you are making on your teacher's notes.

The number of points you will be making is up to you. But, it should be appropriate for the time you have during the session to cover each point (Your primary teaching verses) along with the comments on verses in between. Do not forget to include time to ask and have the question answered by the students. When they are engaged they are truly open for learning.

Preparation is important to organize your thoughts as well as determine the flow of the study. Remember, it is the quality of the journey that makes for a good teaching experience. Do not rush it or feel pressed to get through a certain amount of material. Your concern is whether or not your group is learning about the Bible. That is the entire purpose of the night.

Know Your Group

Because of facilitating, a leader has a tremendous opportunity to evaluate the people in the class. When you ask a question, you can note who answered it on your teacher's notes. This is used later to examine the types of questions that people respond to. If more people respond to easier questions that are more of an obvious nature because the answer is right in the text, you may want to increase the number of these types of questions. If on the other hand, people answered more when they involved a life lesson, you may want to ask more of those types of questions. This can vary depending on the make-up of the class as it involves personal preferences and amount of Biblical knowledge people have in the class.

Knowing your members of the group better, by evaluating their answers, helps you pinpoint weaknesses in their knowledge or ideas. When you get into studies that will point up an area that someone needs to understand more fully, you can put in a few more questions. In this way no one knows that anyone needs help. It is just questions that are being asked. Using the facilitating method of teaching is a win-win all the way around.

The way a leader responds to the questions and answers the students give is important also. Most of the time I try not to come out and say a person is wrong in their answers and never treat any question as stupid or in any way disrespectful. Sometimes they may say the wrong answer that also gives people the wrong idea of a Biblical concept. This still must be handled in a way that doesn't hurt anyone feelings. But, it is important to straighten out any misconceptions.

The Benefit of Deviation

As study leaders, we want to make sure we stay on track with the lessons, but deviations are bound to occur in open discussions. While it is important to stay on track to the studies goal, we must not lose sight of the ultimate goal of realizing God's love. Therefore, it is appropriate to follow deviations before bringing the study back on track,

To give you an example, I usually have points in every lesson that I asked about that are directly answered in the text. Let us say we were talking about John 3:16. It starts out "For God so loved the world that He gave His only Son ..." The question on the student sheet says, why did God give His only Son? ...". Someone raises their hand and says, "to abolish the Law". The answer is not correct from what the text in the lesson says. The correct answer is "For God so loved the world". He gave His son because He loved us. The answer is also not correct from what the Bible says elsewhere. Matthew 5:17 explicitly says He did not come to abolish the Law. So, in this instance it requires me to deviate from my lesson to correct the notion Christ came to "abolish the Law" as well as to get back to the point of the lesson. The point of the lesson was to talk about God's extreme love for us and how we can know it.

So, you see that deviations may need to be answered in a little deeper way. This will require taking a side trip, like in this case about the answer concerning "abolishing the Law". Remember the idea that you are in a nice conversation with friends and you are gently talking with them when correcting this person. You might also make a note of the misconception to be used later in another study to reinforce the correct idea.

There is a good chance that you will have to take side trips away from planned lessons often. This makes the preparation for the lesson itself important. By doing due diligence in getting ready for the night's study, you will have no trouble getting back to the planned lesson from any unscheduled trips.

Have a Good Time

I enjoy all the classes that I have done or am doing right now. The reason is that we talk with each other. Being a facilitator is a great experience, it takes the pressure off everyone in the class. The students are at ease and so is the teacher. In this method, it breaks the barrier of the teacher student down to just friends talking with a person who is helping move the conversation along. With the preparation mentioned the leader becomes the default person, or rather the "go to" person, when the verses need clarification, or the conversation takes a wrong turn. My biggest thrill is when ideas are being exchanged and my part in it is minimal. The class is learning not only how to read the Bible with discernment of ideas, but also they understand more of the bigger picture of how the Bible fits together.

Good preparation enables you as the teacher, to have a great night and enjoy the teaching experience too! As you tie each of these chapters together you will see the plan come together. Becoming proficient at giving Bible studies is immensely rewarding. I think you'll find it surprisingly easy and wonderfully satisfying.

Preparation for a class on _____Date_____

Current events to introduce ideas that coincide with the lesson (To be brought up as normal conversations where appropriate):

_____
_____
_____

Prayer requests from preceding weeks to ask people about:

_____
_____
_____

New Prayer Requests (to bring to the group):

_____
_____

Prayer:

Comments of verses leading to a key verse:

_____
_____

Verse:

Point to be made:

Back up commentaries and correlate other verses

_____
_____

Comments on verses in between points to be made

_____
_____

Verse:

Point to be made:

Back up commentaries and correlate other verses

_____
_____

Comments on verses in between points to be made

_____
_____

Verse:

Point to be made:

Back up commentaries and correlate other verses:
_____
_____

Summary of the night's lessons
_____
_____
_____
_____
_____

Take-away for class to talk about
_____
_____
_____
_____

The Chapter VII

"They asked each other, "Were not our hearts burning within us while he talked with us on the road and opened the Scriptures to us?" (NIV Luke 24:32)

Eliminate Boring Bible Studies

We all have attended meetings, some tremendous and others not as good. Bible Studies are no different. I've talked with people after Bible studies and for the ones that were not as good, I of course, heard negative comments. For those studies, I made some mental notes on how things could have been changed. Some negative comments were that they just did not understand ideas in the Bible. Others have said they do not understand how they can relate the message to today. Still others have said it was hard to stay awake during the lesson. But, for the most part, it seemed to boil down to the people attending and the atmosphere that they felt was at the Bible study itself. Certainly, the study is important but setting the stage is crucial for a students' first impression, which often sets the tone for the night.

As for the study itself, a lot of people might agree with the statement that "One of the driest subjects to study is the Bible". There are reasons that the Bible can appear dry. But, I can tell you that the Bible is the most exciting and awe-inspiring book that has ever been written. It is never the Bible's fault. If a study is not well received, it is usually because the people lost interest in actually studying the Bible, the mood and atmosphere of the study was not good, or the leader needs help in attracting people and making it interesting once people come to the study.

-Brent Mackey

Setting the Stage/Great Expectations

When we talk about setting the stage, there is more to it than just inviting "would be students" to your home. Everyone has an expectation when going to a Bible study. Some of the things that people expect or look forward to at a Bible study are camaraderie with fellow Christians, an opportunity to show what a person knows about the Bible already, exposure to new ideas, to learn more about the Bible itself, food, and/or a bit of fun. If something is new and expands their thinking, it becomes very memorable. If during the Bible study they can feel good about themselves by contributing something that others genuinely appreciate, they will talk about it for weeks and even years.

As a leader, knowing what people are looking for in a study can help you to set the stage to fulfill these expectations. It will pay off if you take into consideration each prospect individually when organizing your lessons.

Camaraderie

Camaraderie is the idea of friendship and good feelings between members of a group. When people get together, they form a specific group. I am always amazed at how many different types of groups there are in any given area. I have met people from groups like:

- Card clubs
- Wood carvers
- Hunters
- Skiers
- And many, many more

Belonging to a group ties people in that group to a certain level of comfort with each other. This comfort grows as time goes on. As they continue to meet, things happen that are memorable, and that memory brings people closer. The same is true for Bible studies. Hopefully, there are other shared good times to add to those memories: things like unexpected visitors, and times that we struggled through the evening for one reason or another. All these types of things contribute to camaraderie. When someone in the group is going through hard times and getting encouragement from the group, it can be rewarding and can build strong bonds with all the people involved. After meeting for a while, these group members have a wonderful bond that is felt whenever they meet.

When we belong to a group that puts a priority on God and His Son, our Lord and Savior Jesus Christ, it is a wonderful feeling. I have come to understand the great tie that Christian brothers and sisters have. The bond we build when learning about the grace and love that God has for us, and how we should be showing that to other people, far exceeds the bond and caring of normal club relationships. The more we learn about the Lord the more there is an instant family relationship with anyone who is a Christian. It is a wonderful, awesome family that God gives us when we get to know Him along with others in this way. This is a big part of eliminating boring Bible Studies. Most people want to see family members or close friends.

Nothing in the meeting seems boring as people laugh and talk about old times. Relationships go a long way in eliminating boredom in a Bible Study.

To encourage this connection within the group a leader can:

- Highlight one person each week to talk about a success or interesting event in his or her life.
- Mention a person's profession and ask a question about it.
- Ask about people's older prayer requests to see what's happening now.
- Have people talk about upcoming events in their lives.
- Bring up things in the past that made the group laugh or have fun.
- Have everyone come early for a cookout before class to interact with each other.
- Explain memories and funny events more fully to newer people when they come up, never leave people out of the loop.

I think you get the idea. Things that will make connection with other people by going through something together and/or knowing things about others bring people closer together.

A potential draw back with this idea is that some people feel the group is perfect the way it is, and no more people are needed. It is imperative to make everyone feel welcome. Be sensitive to including everyone in the conversations preceding the actual study. We want new people to feel they are part of our group.

The Leader's Ego

There is a little difference between a family and a Bible study. In a Bible study there is no extreme father figure. The teacher is kind of like a father in terms of showing people new ideas and helping them learn. However, not like a father in terms of being in any way overbearing. The leader is a facilitator not a stern schoolmaster. We treat each other as brothers and sisters – everyone is on an equal footing. Of course, the teacher/facilitator should have more knowledge of the study and come prepared. This makes him or her the leader, but not a ruler over the students. It's kind of a balancing act. So, the way to conduct the Bible study is in reverence and love, respecting everyone while, at the same time, motivating them toward having a wonderful Bible study.

Therefore, a teacher's ego has no place in a Bible study. Students should not be afraid to help the teacher out by questioning a point or a statement that seems wrong. If someone happens to question you during a study, make sure that any correction offered is right. By taking the time to look up Scriptures and verify the correct answer, it validates the question as legitimate and teaches the class how to deal with any concerns of accuracy. It also shows the class how important it is to check out Biblical details properly.

I just saw a friend of mine that had been in my Bible study for over ten years. As always, the instant family feeling takes over and we reminisced for a while. We had a great time. We talked about how different people reacted to the same study and remembered the food and the interaction between people. But, eventually he said to me "remember the time that you said that the demons went into 1000 swine and I said they went into 2000? And I was right. "We laughed and I told him that he did such a great job of checking on the facts for me.

One of the rules that I always tell the students is to check me out and disagree or correct me if necessary. But, this incident happened 6 or 7 years earlier. He still remembered very clearly about the night he was able to help me and correct me. It's funny about humans; we like to remember the time when our light shone in a given situation. I usually get remarks like that when I meet a person after being away from each other a while. I love reliving those happy memories with them.

If you are leading a Bible study and a question is asked that you don't know or are unsure of, open the question up to the students. And sometimes if a question is asked and you do know the answer- open it up to the students anyway. The incident about a student remembering he corrected me 7 years before really drove the point home for me. People like a little lime light. When they get an opportunity to answer a question and do it well the limelight lasts so much longer than you as the teacher may ever realize. But, they will most definitely be back to the study.

Asking students to help me out if they know the answer has led to great opportunities to encourage the students. Here's a great thought to remember for the teacher wanting to keep people coming to the Bible study:

If someone is able to correctly answer a question that comes up in a Bible study, he or she will want to come back next week!

What does food have to do with boring Bible Studies?

Another thing that can make a difference is having food to eat during the Bible study. Although I always had a lot of food, it is not necessary to have an abundance of different kinds of food. Making it available during the study is a draw that can cause people to come back. Eating is a comforting activity that relaxes people. It also gives them something to do without drawing attention to themselves. It's also something people do with friends and family. It becomes natural for people who share food together to draw closer and build friendships. Sometimes if a part of the study is not appealing to someone or they already know the verse well that you are discussing, reaching for something to eat keeps them from being bored.

The day after Jesus fed the 5000, He called them out about wanting to follow Him just because people wanted food. Food is a draw and people will come for that. Jesus also told the people to "work for the food that endures to eternal life" (See John 6:26). But nonetheless, preparing some nice snack type food and drinks will be well received. It will draw people to come for the next Bible study.

Having Fun

In addition, People love to enjoy themselves and have a little fun too. How can you have fun at a Bible study of all things? Usually, it is the chemistry of the people at the Bible study that makes it a great experience. Charismatic out-going people make a big difference in the mix of students. A leader who is well versed in the Bible but not outgoing needs to have a sidekick who is friendly and personable (Perhaps a good friend or spouse).

Have you ever been to a party and been bored? I've been to several parties where it seems dead – no life at all. Then someone arrives and the entire party changes with the arrival of that one person who gets things going. S/he Joins in the group and talks with everyone and maybe hams it up just a little. Or s/he will come in and tell a joke and people start to laugh and talk with each other. At that point, people let down their guard and can have a good time. When people are being real and not putting on a façade it becomes fun.

Now, once that happens in the Bible study people feel free enough with the group to ask questions or make comments (Even if a few are a little funny – never irreverent or sacrilegious though). This makes the evening fun and not restrictive and stiff. I had one of the men tell me he had a gutter cleaning guy who only charged him 25.00. He said everyone else wanted 75.00 to 100.00. He said he did for him for a few years and then he just dropped out of sight and he didn't know where he went. I said I know where went – bankrupt. Everyone laughed and the room became alive.

So, learning can be funny sometimes too. In another study, one of my closer friends told us that over the weekend traveling on the turnpike he was passing another car and a man came up behind him and started honking his horn wanting him to go faster. He said the guy was being a real jerk, so he matched his speed to the car he was passing and slowed down and made the jerk have to go even slower. He said the guy got so mad that he went on the shoulder to go around him and my friend said the stakes that denote portions of a mile were slapping the hood of the guy's car as they broke off while he tried to pass. Everyone was laughing and my close friend was getting a kick out of himself. So, I said I have one question for you. He said what? I said, "Did the guy get to the hospital in time to say goodbye to his dying wife?" For a few seconds there was complete silence. My friend looked at me and said, "You're a jerk". Then everyone started laughing.

I prefaced this story saying that it was my close friend because if it was someone new, I would have used a little different approach. But, the point I wanted make is that there could have been another reason, other than being a jerk, for why he was acting that way. The man may have had a purpose for it. Let's treat others the way we want to be treated. I did it with a joke that my friend remembers (Also others that were there) to this day. My point was driven home, and I don't believe my friend would do that again without thinking first back to that study.

Bible studies can be a lot of fun especially if people know that the leader cares about each and every one of the people attending. Constructive remarks can be made without them being construed as destructive comments. Kidding can be done because they know that you love them and mean them no harm. As a matter of fact, sometimes people want to be kidded. It means they are one of the group, just as long as it's not overdone or always kidding the same person. Just remember, do not do that sort of thing with new people. The love part comes with getting to know the leader and feeling the love and compassion. Without that, it just becomes a cruel.

Warming Up the Group

The beginning part of any Bible study is a time when people have just arrived, and the Bible study has not officially started. This period should be a time that gets people warmed up for the evening. If you are a leader and find yourself having a hard time "warming up" the group here are a couple of suggestions:

1. Start out with a Bible quiz – this quiz is only for fun and people don't even need to take the quiz – they can just mark the right answers as you read them off

for the rest who did take the quiz. It needs to be a short 10-15 question test (Multiple-choice) and give them about 5 minutes or less to write down the answers. The internet is a tremendous source in finding sites that offer this type of questions and they usually come with the answers.

2. Tell a joke – if it doesn't go over allow yourself to be the brunt of the "stupid joke" remarks. Laugh and take it all in good fun. The object is to get everyone feeling comfortable talking to each other even if it's about your unfunny joke.

3. Talk about an issue that has come up lately concerning a topic on which everyone will have their own opinions. Then discuss how it should be handled. Stay away from overly controversial subjects that could cause dissention. Choose subjects that have to do with things like sports decisions or games, fashion designs, someone who got fired publicly, someone who was recently promoted, new restaurants opening etc. The idea is to get everyone to join in giving an opinion. Remember to keep it to a subject that cannot be hotly contested or argued about to any extreme.

4. Situational problems that someone in the group has and needs help in deciding what to do. These are always very productive conversations because the group can take Biblical principles and apply them to real situations.

The warm-up time is exactly what it sounds like. Just as coming in from the cold and we need to get the blood flowing, the same thing applies to our brains. Just arriving, our mind set may be on the slippery roads, the day's big problem, or a conversation over the phone before coming. Any number of things could be confronting us. Everyone (Even the leader) needs to calm down and get the mood set for a great evening.

How can I get the Bible Study Started?

Timing is important on these types of warm-ups. Remember, they are in a Bible study to learn about the Bible. Sometimes I will let a subject go on until everyone has had a least one thing to say but, never more than 10- or 12-minutes tops. Below are some ideas of how to end the warmup period.

1. Ok, let me have one more comment on this topic, then let's go to prayer time, and get things rolling.
2. Why don't we include this in our prayer tonight and get some guidance from the Lord? Who else has something they want us to pray about tonight?
3. Well, I guess we've just about beaten that topic up to a pulp – any prayer requests tonight?
4. Ok everybody, that's a topic that we could talk about all night so if you want to - let's pick it up next week and go to prayer time now - for tonight.
5. With that comment, let's fill our coffee cups and get to the study.

Setting the stage, or warming up, is designed to help people get relaxed and so it should be a little freewheeling for a few minutes. When people are relaxed, they tend to be in a good frame of mind and a very receptive mood for Bible study.

Learning More Concerning the Bible Itself

There are Bibles that are apologetically focused. These Bibles give insight on how different sections of the Bible applied to the culture, science, language and archeological finds. These are wealth of information that you can use to inform the class about interesting facts. Appearing as pages between chapters the facts and ideas are very easy to understand. This will give you some ideas of things to interject as you do studies, things not commonly known.

Commentaries will do the same thing. But, its more focused on literal words as opposed to telling you things like what an early church father may have said, or what a boat may have looked like or why the issue of Jesus touching a leper was so different than what we think of today. These come as small insights that don't require a lot of time to tell people. We don't want to take much time out of our class to expand on these types of things. However, it can be adding a little salt to the mix. Make it a little more interesting.

Studying the Bible should bring out interesting facts by just studying the pages themselves. For instance, when we read Jonah, we find he did not want to do what God ask of him. He was to go to Nineveh and preach. He didn't want to go and boarded a ship to go the opposite way. God made a big fish to swallowed Jonah and spit him up on the shore of Nineveh. That event has many great points to be brought up. Jonah's rebellion even though he was so close to God helps us see that we have company sometimes we can get a little messed up too.

But people for a long time said it was a great story to illustrate that we should always do what God wants us to do. Not being defiant like Jonah. Look what happened to him. I'm being simplistic to make a different point. People thought it was just a fanciful book and the Nineveh didn't even exist. That Jonah and the whale was just an instructional made-up story.

However, interjecting things like archeologists discovered Nineveh by finding a stone with Jonah's name on it makes people think about it a little. If that part of Jonah has been verified, how did Jonah get to Nineveh? He was on a ship going the opposite way. There had to be a way Jonah went to the largest city in Assyria. He also must have done something for them to make a huge stone carving in his honor. Why would they even listen to him to begin with? They were enemies. Could it be that he looked like he'd been in the belly of a fish for 3 days perhaps? Interesting points! How would he have even gotten to the king let alone talk with him, unless there was something very different about him.

The Bible has always been found true and accurate. Archeologists use the Bible when they're digging in that region as a key source of information. It has proven to be the most factual source of information for Archeologists. When information like this about the Bible is brought out, people talk about it with their friends. The more people study the Bible the more they learn about the wisdom and truth contained in it. We, as teachers, need to bring out these different facts about the Bible.

The entire Bible is written to bring us closer to God. The miracles Jesus did brought people to listen to Him and eventually worship God. Through Christ, they learned of God's love and grace. We are not able to raise the dead or do the miracles that Jesus did. But, the Bible is a miraculous book. By showing the miracles of fore knowledge and prophecy coupled with the story of Jesus and His love for us and His sacrifice for us, people draw closer to Christ and God. The Gift of the Holy Spirit makes these things ring true to us. Understanding and growing close to God is the reason we study the Bible and it's the reason we teach the Bible. It's the miracle that we have to show people and get them to listen to the Gospel Story.

As you read through the pages of this book my hope is that you will understand some of the wonder I behold when I read the Bible. Moreover, the joy I have been given every time I teach it to others.

New Ideas New Concepts

Keeping the study from being boring can come in many forms. One way is to keep your mind as well as the students minds open for new ideas or concepts. People love to learn new ideas. There is a little light bulb that goes off in a person's head when they realize a new concept or way of looking at something. That realization also opens pathways that touch a lot of other ideas and applications. Like a pebble thrown in the water, the waves touch a lot of things that people don't even realize.

If a leader looks closely at the Scriptures, many times fresh new ideas can be brought out. Done correctly, it will tie reasons and logic together in such a way that the students sense a spark of enlightenment going off in their heads. That is such a tremendous feeling and one that energizes students. It makes them want to come back to get more of the same experiences in the next study.

Sometimes we will hit on a verse that the commentators are not settled on. Or they are just not clear on. This is an excellent time to ask the class what they think could be going on in the verse. This will give them an opportunity to give their own ideas on the subject. A student should always be able to comment on an idea of their own, even if they differ from the commentators. However, when that happens we must explore a few ways to handle it, depending on the circumstances. Generally, the idea, if it differs widely with other commentators, will be wrong. However, sometimes the person could actually bring up some great points to consider. Therefore, handling the situation becomes more of gently getting into the subject always being ready to take the time to tell a person they have the wrong slant on the subject at hand. Here are some tips:

First, acknowledge the fact that you as the leader love the class because people are free thinkers and willing to step out and bring new ideas. From there:

- Before discussion begins on someone's idea, everyone that wants to comment needs to have a supporting verse(s) that backs up their view concerning that new idea.
- No one is right or wrong at this point until all parties are heard.
- We can, at the end of the discussion, agree to disagree.
- Commentaries from other sources can be read (As long as it's not overly long).
- At the end of a reasonable time the leader will give his/her point of view
- If the initiator of the idea is incorrect that's ok – ideas and discussion are what it's all about. We as a group should always be thankful for people who are brave enough to

put forth new ideas. Without people being able to contribute their thoughts there never would be any new ideas. But, in this case the Bible in other verses points to a different slant. However, the time is well spent because the correct idea will be cemented in our minds because of the discussion.

- If the initiator is right or even could be right, then we applaud him/her for coming forward with such a novel and unique idea.

The leader must take the role of judge/mediator in these instances. As such, time may be needed for you to consult someone or something else concerning the issue before your bringing more facts to the class. The same applies to the idea of people getting too involved and getting upset. Time to agree to disagree or move on until more information can be obtained by the leader. In some instances, you might bring someone that you respect to the class to answer the question. But, generally, it's just a nice 5- or 10-minute break from going over verses. I have had people that get too invested in the discussion. In those cases, I take the person aside and tell them that they know too much and the people that don't know as much can't follow. Nevertheless, I want to hear what they have to say and so I'll stay a few minutes after class to talk about it. I stay and listen to them. When you are alone with people who have been a little too passionate, they have had a chance to cool down and without an audience they are much more reasonable.

Mad people are seldom reasonable and reasonable people are seldom mad.

Cancel the Study

Finally, don't be afraid to cancel a study. People come to learn about the Bible and a leader must not lose sight of that goal. Always plan a good lesson and come to every Bible study ready to teach. If before a Bible study everything is just going wrong and you really will not be prepared to teach, it is better to cancel. People have something better to do than to waste a night without accomplishing anything. However too many cancellations and you will lose people. So try your best not to cancel your studies.

Chapter VIII

"13 What you heard from me, keep as the pattern of sound teaching, with faith and love in Christ Jesus. 14 Guard the good deposit that was entrusted to you—guard it with the help of the Holy Spirit who lives in us."
(NIV 2Timothy 1:13)

Formulating Book Bible Studies

When I was younger, I was enthralled with the way that speakers could get up and deliver a speech. It was engaging and it seemed so passionate and heartfelt. It was the same for entertainers. How they could "wow" the audience and captivate them while they were on stage. They could respond to the audience "adlibbing" to someone's response. I thought they must be exceptionally quick witted to be able to respond as quickly as they do. That was until I realized that the passion and "adlibs" were written into a script.

They must have practiced a lot to sound so genuine every time they delivered the same "show" night after night. Even down to coughs and looking surprised. It also happened when I went twice the same Sunday to a church with multiple church services. I noticed the same applied to teacher's teaching the same lesson. I quickly realized that to do something well for a group or even a single person requires forethought and practice.

When I give a Bible study today, I go through my old notes, refresh them, and practice the study. I will practice and re read it several times before giving it. I feel more confident about the information to be discussed and the best way to deliver it.

-Brent Mackey

The object of this chapter is to give clear, easy steps to follow in preparing for a Bible study. The goal is to encourage every leader to take the time and effort to own the study. By knowing the steps to accomplish writing and giving a good study, students will be encouraged to listen and come to your classes.

First Things First

Consider the bible study you want to conduct. First, take into consideration the Bible studies (if any) you have already given as well as the group dynamics before deciding whether the next study will be a topical one or a book of the Bible. Both Bible studies focus on the Bible but are different in how the students perceive and understand the study itself. A book study will concern itself with mainly the group of Scriptures in a set place in the Bible and with a set group of purposes or topics. Although a book may have been written for a larger general idea, there will be many topics and subtopics to discuss. For most of the study you would then be in one book as a primary area of study. The teaching will concern itself with a specific people, history, poetry, prophecies, time, or problems needing to be addressed.

In the case of letters in the New Testament, they were written to help with application and understanding of God's word and Christ's message. In comparison, a topical study which uses chain references to look at different perspectives in different places throughout the Bible about the same subject. This may involve several passages in different books sometimes from beginning to the end of the Bible. It will have different resources with changing environments such as time written, author, and culture at the time of writing. We will find these things as we look at the topic throughout different books in the Bible that span over approximately a 2000-year period.

Next, consider how you will formulate the study. This can be fun and extremely rewarding for the teacher/leader. You can use a premade Bible study, but consider making your own. It is a little more time-consuming, but the benefits are worth the extra time. Being directly involved with the purpose will naturally result in a deeper understanding for you as the leader as your mind remains open to new considerations throughout the study. You can also have a mixture of a readymade study and extra material that you have inserted. Either way the leader needs to have the goal be - making a well thought out and prepared plan for each lesson.

Introduction Preparation: History

Let us look at a Bible "book" study. Once you have picked the book to study, the next thing to do is to get the history of the book to obtain information for the introduction and general purpose the book was written. It is helpful to give students the setting and culture for them to get their imagination working. The study becomes more memorable if they have pictures in their minds as they read the words and answer questions. Matthew Henry is a particularly good source for information on the total Bible. It is also economical as it is usually offered with other programs for a minimal cost if not free. Here is a sample of a history portion of Matthew Henry's commentary for 1st Corinthians in which, during my own study, I would underline what I want to tell my own students.

An Exposition, with Practical Observations, of The First Epistle of St. Paul to the Corinthians[3]

Corinth was a principal city of Greece, in that particular division of it which was called Achaia. It was situated on the isthmus (or neck of land) that joined Peloponnesus to the rest of Greece. They traded to Italy and the west and Asia. From this situation, it is no wonder that Corinth should be a place of great trade and wealth; and, as affluence is apt to produce luxury of all kinds, neither is it to be wondered at if a place so famous for wealth and arts should be infamous for vice. It was in a particular manner noted for fornication, insomuch that a Corinthian woman was a proverbial phrase for a strumpet, and korinthiazein, korinthiasesthai - to play the Corinthian, is to play the whore, or indulge whorish inclinations. Yet in this lewd city did Paul, by the blessing of God on his labors, plant and raise a Christian church, chiefly among the Gentiles, as seems very probable from the history of this matter, Acts 18:1-18, compared with some passages in this epistle, particularly 1 Co_12:2, where the apostle tells them, You know that you were Gentiles, carried away to those dumb idols even as you were led, though it is not improbable that many Jewish converts might be also among them, for we are told that Crispus, the chief ruler of the synagogue, believed on the Lord, with all his house, Act_18:8. He continued in this city nearly two years, as is plain from Act_18:11 and Act_18:18 compared, and labored with great success, being encouraged by a divine vision assuring him God had much people in that city, Act_18:9, Act_18:10. Nor did he use to stay long in a place where his ministry met not with acceptance and success.

Sometime after he left them he wrote this epistle to them, to water what he had planted and rectify some gross disorders which during his absence had been introduced. And it is but too visible how much their wealth had helped to corrupt their manners, from the several faults for which the apostle reprehends them. Pride, avarice, luxury, lust (the natural offspring of a carnal and corrupt mind), are all fed and prompted by outward affluence. Their pride discovered itself in their parties and factions, and the notorious disorders they committed in the exercise of their spiritual gifts. Their luxury appeared in more instances than one, in their dress, in their debauching themselves even at the Lord's table.

It is manifest from this state of things that there was much that deserved reprehension, and needed correction, in this church. And the apostle, under the direction and influence of the Holy Spirit, sets himself to do both with all wisdom and faithfulness, and with a due mixture of tenderness and authority, as became one in so elevated and important a station in the church. After a short introduction at the beginning of the epistle, he first blames them for their discord and factions, enters into the

---

[3] Excerpts taken from Matthew Henry's Commentary on the Whole Bible- New Testament by Matthew Henry (Public Domain)

origin and source of them, shows them how much pride and vanity, and the affectation of science, and learning, and eloquence, flattered by false teachers, contributed to the scandalous schism; and prescribes humility, and submission to divine instruction, the teaching of God by his Spirit, both by external revelation and internal illumination, as a remedy for the evils that abounded amongst them.

Remember, reading from a paper or book is very boring. So, read different commentaries and underline important ideas. Get a cue of what to say by noticing the underlined portions and then describe in more detail what you have read previously. This enables you to have an atmosphere of just talking with students and not reading to them. It becomes much more effective and if a question comes up you can still refer to the entire text to quickly read over to find the answer if you do not remember it from your reading prior to the study.

The object of a Bible study's first lesson is to give a quick overview of what is to be covered in the study. The overview should be interesting and give a glimpse of the setting in which the text was written. This will help the students to gain some understanding about the feelings and situations confronting the people involved in the writings. This is not necessarily the time for the teacher to ask questions, it is the time for putting the minds of everyone in the class on the time period and circumstances of the people to whom the letter is written (In this case, those reading the letter at the time were mostly the Corinthians).

Introduction Preparation: Items to be covered

We are so lucky today to have the internet and programs we can buy that cover all the things we need to make a great Bible study. Some are economically priced, and others are more expensive. At times, you will need to lean on some of the resources heavily. Other times you will have covered the ideas and studies before and can use your own notes.

Below is a commentary by Adam Clarke, from Commentary on the Bible, (Public Domain) one of several commentators.

> Analysis of the First Epistle to the Corinthians
> *This epistle, as to its subject matter, has been variously divided: into three parts by some; into four, seven, eleven, etc., parts, by others. Most of these divisions are merely artificial, and were never intended by the apostle. The following seven particulars comprise the whole: -*
> I.   *The Introduction, 1Co_1:1-9.*
> II. *Exhortations relative to their dissensions, 1 Corinthians 1:9-4:21.*

III. *What concerns the person who had married his step-mother, commonly called the incestuous person, 1Co_5:1-13, 6, and 7.*

IV. *The question concerning the lawfulness of eating things which had been offered to idols, 1Co_8:1-13, 9, and 10, inclusive.*

V. *Various ecclesiastical regulations, 1 Corinthians 11-14, inclusive.*

VI. *The important question concerning the resurrection of the dead, 1 Corinthians 15.*

VII. *Miscellaneous matters; containing exhortations, salutations, commendations, etc., etc., 1 Corinthians 16.*

Armed with the information above it becomes quite easy to explain to the class the different things that will be covered in 1st Corinthians. It is good to reference Adam Clarke's points as they come up during the chapters as you come to them. It reinforces the information in the people's minds.

As you can see, these programs are of great value to teaching a class on the Bible. "Copy and paste" function makes it much easier to prepare the teacher notes. I always consult a few commentaries to determine the best and clearest information to use for the class. I have also used parts of different commentaries and put them together to make a more complete picture for the total introduction.

Preparing the Study for the First Chapter

The first chapter of every book is unique in comparison with the rest of the study. Not only is it the start of the book that gives information concerning the audience and the author it also sets the tone for the entire book. We must pay special attention to the details that are important to the tone of the book. This will help people today journey back and experience some of what the early audience would have experienced. This is often done at the same time the historical view is given.

Preparing the Study for Other Chapters

Now we need to prepare and formulate the actual Bible study itself. Usually I work with one chapter at a time per class. This is not etched in stone because some chapters are small, and more information can be covered in a 1-hour class than a small chapter. At other times one chapter may need more time than just 1 hour. We need to be flexible. Often, I will have two chapters with me in case more than one is needed. Remember the important idea to a Bible study is the journey not the speed. Making the pages of the Bible come to life is about an experience. Take the time to make it enjoyable.

Now there are several different programs that help a Bible study teacher with very fundamental routine questions. These programs can help you get started on the Bible study and as you read these questions, they may help you gain a direction to take for questions that go deeper into a subject. Let me give you an example of what fundamental routine questions are.

Let us look at the Gospel of John. The book of John differs from 1st Corinthians because John is a historical account of Jesus as well as containing a tremendous amount of truth, prophecies, and fulfillment of prophecies from the Old Testament. It was written so that all Christians would know about the Lord and was not focused on one group's problems.

Let us look at the beginning of John chapter 10. I pick chapter 10 because it lends itself to good expansion on several issues. And hopefully will take a student on an interesting and fruitful study time.

First, just for clarification, the introduction for the class would already have been given at the start of the Gospel of John and does not need to be repeated at this time. People would have been well into this book as nine chapters have already been studied.

The first question:

1. What are some of the ways we can tell whether something is genuine or not? (A generic opening question to get people to talk about one of the subjects to be discussed using their own background. This is not a Biblical question – it is a life experience question)

On to the study for the night:

Sometimes the previous chapter is important to the context of the chapter being studied. This is because the bible chapters and numbers were given at random. They were just meant to allow some sort of reference points to find the different parts of the Bible easily. These reference points were given much later (Some theologians say as late as the twelfth century) and have little bearing on when a thought or idea stops and starts. Often the previous chapter or a part of the chapter needs to be reviewed to give the needed context for the next chapter's Bible study. With that in mind we need to give the students a little explanation about the situation from chapter 9 – we will call that "the setup."

The Setup:

A man, who was healed by the Lord, defended Him to the religious leaders and was thrown out of the temple. Below are the scriptures (Studied the previous week) just before our text:

> "Jesus heard that they had thrown him out, and
> when he found him, he said, "Do you believe in the
> Son of Man?"
> "Who is he, sir?" the man asked. "Tell me so that I
> may believe in him."
> Jesus said, "You have now seen him; in fact, he is
> the one speaking with you."
> Then the man said, "Lord, I believe," and he
> worshiped him.
> Jesus said, "For judgment I have come into this
> world, so that the blind will see and those who see
> will become blind."
> Some Pharisees who were with him heard him say
> this and asked, "What? Are we blind too?"
> Jesus said, "If you were blind, you would not be
> guilty of sin; but now that you claim you can see,
> your guilt remains."
> (NIV John 9:35-41)

Now to the text we are going to talk about for the study:

> "I tell you the truth, the man who does not enter the
> sheep pen by the gate, but climbs in by some other
> way, is a thief and a robber. The man who enters by
> the gate is the shepherd of his sheep. The watchman
> opens the gate for him, and the sheep listen to his
> voice. He calls his own sheep by name and leads
> them out. When he has brought out all his own, he
> goes on ahead of them, and his sheep follow him
> because they know his voice. But, they will never
> follow a stranger; in fact, they will run away from
> him because they do not recognize a stranger's
> voice."
> (NIV John 10:1-5)

1. Who did Jesus say was a thief and a robber? (10:1)

2. What kind of relationship do sheep have with their shepherd? (10:2-4)
3. Why won't sheep follow a stranger? (10:5)

This is very similar to many of the Bible study question books that are available. As you can see, it asks basic questions and is an exceptionally good starting point for the Bible study. The questions can be easily found in the text. Getting to the next question is where the work begins.

The context in chapter 9's verses gives us the needed information to determine that the Lord is talking about something bigger than just shepherding in the beginning of chapter 10. In this case the Lord is using real things to illustrate something else. It is an allegory. An allegory (parable) is the expression of certain characteristics, situations or facts about human conduct and experience using symbolic fictional objects, figures and actions.

Jesus used this type of story quite often. The story in John 10:1-5 is a story that represents something other than the actual figures used in the story. Jesus used these types of stories to illustrate a truth that becomes evident to the listener as the facts are brought out. Then, the realization of the application of the story becomes apparent.

The Questions:

Realizing John's passage was an allegory, what kind of questions do you have concerning the different characters and objects in John's passages about the sheep pen? Your questions will be the same as those trying to learn more in the Bible study. You as the leader will need to supply the answers. Here are some thoughts:

First, each person mentioned must represent something else. Who do we have in the story? Thief and a robber, the man who enters the gate, the watchman who opens the gate for him, the sheep and a stranger all have an important part to play. Wouldn't you like to know whom all these figures represented?

What about the situations – entering the sheep pen by climbing in some other way. What about following the shepherd? What about recognizing voices?

So, we have a lot to ask questions about in these verses and perhaps we do not have all the answers. We may find ourselves in a situation that the questions are stumping us. What can we do? We can go to commentaries and try to find the answers to the questions that we do not have the answers for. It is also good to check the answer you think you have right just to see if anyone ever thought of it the way you did. Make sure you, as the teacher, rightly discern the Word of God. It is one of THE MOST important aspects of a teacher or Bible study leader.[4]

If you are a pastor, you most likely know someone to ask in times of uncertainty over a Biblical passage. If you are not, then talk to your pastor. I have been incredibly lucky; I have a pastor that is a great resource. Do not feel that it takes away from you as a teacher; your reliable sources appreciate your desire for the right answer. They may even ask you occasionally what you think.

As in the above passages, we can think of good questions on our own. More in-depth questions help make students think about relevant issues. If you have a question, there is every reason to believe that your students will have the same one. So then, to really make a Bible study great, you need to invest your mind and your curiosity. The types of questions that stimulate people's minds are the thought provoking questions that at first are hard to answer. Come up with unique thoughtful questions along with the "in your face" type obvious questions. This will satisfy both ends of your student's learning curve. Although the list below may seem easy, sometimes every question on the list is thought provoking. Concerning the passage being studied:

1. Who is talking?
2. Who is the audience?
3. What was being said?
4. How would the audience in that day have been impacted?
5. What are the implications for today?
6. Is there a hidden meaning (like an analogy, or metaphor or simile)?
7. Does this satisfy a prophecy?
8. Is this a prophecy about the future?
9. Is there an application to our daily life (if so, what is it)?
10. What changes should you make in your life knowing about the application?
11. How does this correlate with other passages in the Bible about the same topic?

---

[4] NOTE OF CAUTION: Make certain that the commentaries agree with the Scriptures. Read enough commentaries from older and newer theologians. You will find some that have a decided slant and they do not really answer the questions. But, usually along the way you will find some that ring true. Just make sure you use a logical approach. If you find four reliable scholars say one thing and then you have only one saying something totally different, you should really investigate more before agreeing with the one that is totally different.

There are countless questions that football off Scripture. The above list should get you started. If you run across a correlation from one Scripture to another Scripture let the students know about it. Also, be ready and willing to have people talk about the questions and expand on the answers. Class participation is where people really can learn a lot. It is also where the students get encouraged by each other. When one makes a good observation or point and receives compliments from the others it makes them feel great and builds them up spiritually.

Pulling it All Together:

As you prepare for the Bible study, make a list of points you feel would be good to make. Sometimes as you go over the questions you may be able to interject important extra Biblical information that would make the verses come alive. However, do not belabor the points, you can say something like "This is just at note about..." or "As a sidelight..." but be brief.

Usually during the course of the Bible study there are some definite points that are uncovered by your questions. Before the Bible study is over try to review the evening's study, either with a wrap up question or with a simple and easy-to-understand recap.

Although I lean on Commentaries to gain insight, please look carefully at the Scripture, and check out points made by a commentator. Check several sources and do not just stick to one writer. Make the Bible study fun and enjoyable by allowing good conversations to involve everyone, while at the same time making sure that good, clear doctrines are not compromised.

In Formulating a Bible study, we have discussed the following points to help you to have a complete Bible study.

- Determine the type of Bible study you are going to give.
- In a book study, the first lesson gives an overview of what is generally happening concerning culture, common concerns, and economy. Extra Biblical books provide some of the information needed as well as correlating Scriptures found in commentaries etc.
- Prepare an easy way for you to go over this information without having to read the other books and articles themselves.
- The start of your questions should be more of getting people in the mood and thinking about what the idea of the chapter is going to be about. So first ask a Life application question.

- When you start a Bible study (after chapter 1), refresh people's memories just a little from the preceding chapter. Limit it to a few sentences just to establish a setting. Where appropriate read a small section of scriptures from the week before.
- Read a section of the chapter you will be studying. Ask simpler questions at first to get things going
- If there is an interesting story or teaching moment that will be interesting to the students, have some fun with it. Do not be too long winded but, some off topic things can loosen up the group.
- Create your Bible study using creative questions and information. Check out all questionable answers to insure correct teaching. Enjoy your opportunity to help people understand the Bible.

Take time to prepare your Bible study it will be worth it.

Chapter IX

"For it is precept upon precept, precept upon
precept, line upon line, line upon line, here a little,
there a little."
(KJV Isaiah 28:10)

Topical and Typological Bible Studies

*When I came across the above scripture, it encapsulated what I had already discovered.
I was 42 years old at the time and had decided that I should give the Bible another try.
Verse building on other verses had been the way I came to believe that the Bible was
truly inspired by God. Topical, typological and even similarities were the backbone of
my belief. These kinds of studies showed me how one scripture can affect another and
how they could even predict future events. If God really existed and wrote the Bible, it
should be a book that would have clues and a certain supremacy that all other books
lacked. It does.*

*Some people do not need to have the Bible proved to be inspired by God. They just
automatically believe it. I'm not one of those people. With diligent study, I felt that I
could be able to get my answer in the pages of the Bible. At first I just came across stories
that were typological as I went through the Bible, later I would search them out.*

*Who but God could inspire a book to be written that would tell of events and furnish
details in the Old Testament that would be identical to other events that would happen
in the New Testament. It could only happen by someone who knew the end from the
beginning. That could only be God. There is no other book like the Bible. Couple these
studies with the fact that the Bible also has clear cut prophecies; you have a book out of
time and space. You have a God given volume that tells us everything we need to know
about life priorities, conduct attitude and most of all His love. His love is exemplified
in Jesus Christ and His death on the cross that opens heavens doors to eternal life with
Him.*

-Brent Mackey

Typological and Topical studies are alike in that they both rely upon
searching in different books for the study. However, Topical studies will
involve more books generally than typological. But, you will find
differences in that, Topical studies tell you about meanings and nuances in
the word structure and/or culture. It tells you about one subject and gives
you an overall knowledge of it as God views it. The supernatural idea of

inspiration rarely occurs in terms of factual information (Scientific areas are one of the exceptions). Whereas Typological studies always have the overriding factor of foreknowledge. As you read about typological things, there's always the natural question "how did the author know?" Then of course you realize that God inspired it to be written (It's the only possible answer aside from sheer coincidence).

What is Typology

Typology is when a person, thing or event (Or combination of these items) in the Old Testament are identified by writings in the New Testament as "types" or are said to be pre-figuring something. When this happens, it is typology. When you read in the Bible (New Testament) the word "as," "like," or "similar" before a sentence, and the description is something in the Old Testament, it is usually typology as well, as in John 3:14:

> **"Just as Moses lifted up the serpent in the desert, so the Son of Man must be lifted up"**
> **(NIV John 3:14)**

> **"And as Moses lifted up the serpent in the wilderness, even so must the Son of man be lifted up"**
> **(KJV John 3:14)**

Some Typological studies can take the entire class to look at and discuss the situation. In which case, I like to say that it can be a stand-alone study. In other words, if someone wants an impromptu lesson, these are great ones to have in your arsenal of studies. It is a study that is informative, shows the inspiration of God, and is easy to show a person the idea of Bible study. At the same time, it's just long enough to engage people without being too long and tedious.

We can also get into typological lessons as we study other things like a book study etc... We invariably come across an area that has a reference to a "type". The example above would come into a study on the book of John the 3rd chapter. We can make a side trip, have a typological study when it comes up, and then return to the book study of John. It makes for very interesting classes by mixing the two at appropriate times.

Typological studies are significant because they bring to light the inspiration of God and teach people that God indeed knows the end from the beginning. Otherwise, it would not be in the Bible. The idea that the Old and New Testaments are tied together as if one mind wrote it is evident. The fact that it was written by over 40 authors, approximately over a 2,000-year period, attests to the awesomeness of God's inspiration and foreknowledge.

In these studies, we need to take care in handling the verses and any comments we teach. It has to be applicable to the events and truths in the New Testament. We do not want to twist scripture to make an idea or fact appear to be a "type" when it isn't clearly visible and understandable. We have to handle with extreme care the Word of God. Someone said, "If it makes common and true sense seek no other sense unless you want nonsense." That is so insightful because it gives us a stopping point for our application of scriptures.

A Biblical Illustration

The below verse starts out by reminding the readers of something that happened in the Old Testament and then tells them that it is like something that happened or is going to happen (and does) in the New Testament. To find out the particulars we have a specific place to look up in the Old Testament. We can then compare the details of the older event to the event that happened in the New Testament.

> **"Just as Moses lifted up the snake in the desert, so the Son of Man must be lifted up, [15] that everyone who believes in him may have eternal life." (NIV John 3:14, 15)**

> **"And as Moses lifted up the serpent in the wilderness, even so must the Son of man be lifted up: That whosoever believeth in him should not perish, but have eternal life." (KJV John 3:14, 15)**

The snake being lifted up is like Christ being lifted up on the cross. To find out where typologies that we already know are located in the Bible, we primarily use a concordance. We look up key words to determine where in the Bible to locate specific words. For the above Biblical illustration, we might look up the word lifted or lift, snake or serpent.[5] In the concordance the word and where it appears in the Bible is listed and also you will find a partial sentence, which will give you the additional information as to what

---

[5] Take into consideration that concordances are written Bible version specific. King James uses serpent New International Version uses snake.

is being lifted. You will be able to see where the event is talked about in the Bible.

Typology vs. Similarities

Typology is the term used when an event or person in the New Testament is clearly identified as pertaining something written in the Old Testament. There are, however, things that appear just a valid as the application of a typology but are not clearly stated as such in the New Testament. If you were to apply the same kind of rules that appear when dealing with a stated typology and it fits, it is a similarity.

Always remember that these types of things in the Old Testament are only a foreshadowing of something in the New Testament. There is no doctrinal value in terms of plowing any new ground or changing things in the New Testament. These "types" foreshadow events, people or things in a way that makes us know God inspires the Bible. It would have to be that way because none other than God would know to include these things in the Old Testament in just the right way to validate the foreknowledge of God. This helps to pave the way for people to realize God knows the end from the beginning. These things only point to Christ and other events; they do not take the place or become more important in any way than the reality of the New Testament occurrence.

These have similar criteria to typology with one exception; the New Testament doesn't identify them as "Types." Therefore, in order to think of things in the Old Testament as being similar and meeting the same criteria as typology we have to ask questions to determine it.

1. Is similar wording used in both verse sections?
2. Is there enough detail to be similar?
3. Is the situation unique enough to make coincidence highly unlikely?
4. Does this validate an excepted principle or concept in the New Testament?
5. If the similarity is doctrinal in nature, it cannot be twisted and stretched as to plow new ground not covered in the New Testament.

The above is just a guideline to help understand that we cannot say everything is similar unless it meets the above criteria. Care must be given to correctly handle the Word of God. There is confusion about typology and similarities between scholars. Some will lump all of the events that qualify for either categories into one under the title "Typology". Others will separate these instances into two groups. The ones talked about in the Old Testament and mentioned as such in the New Testament are called typology. Whereas the instances talked about in the Old Testament that are not mentioned in the New Testament, but could meet the qualifications otherwise, are called similarities (or similar). I choose to use the second method creating two categories. My thinking on this idea is if God inspired the writers to mention specific things pointing back to the Old Testament, it would be a good idea to separate them from ideas not mentioned as "types" in the New Testament.

One of the most glaring examples of a similarity (not mentioned in the New Testament as a "type") is the story about Abraham taking Isaac up the mountain to be sacrificed. This event is similar to God giving up His Son to be crucified. As you read through the details of the event spoken of in Genesis, you will notice a tremendous amount of similarities to Jesus and His heavenly Father as a father (Abraham) takes his son (Isaac) to be a sacrifice. From the miracle birth (neither woman was supposed to be able to become pregnant), to the ram caught in the thicket (Jesus wearing a crown of thorns); there are just too many "coincidental" occurrences to be "coincidental." A full Bible study with student's sheets and teacher's notes can be found in the appendix Bible study #4.

Typology and similarities are both great learning tools to teach students about the foreknowledge of God in the Bible. By noticing details, it becomes plain to see that the things included in the story of the event are exactly or very similar or are allegorical to Christ's life and what He did.[6]

What is a Topical Bible Study?

A Topical Study is geared towards a more generalized topic. It could be a word study, or an area study. For example, the study could cover the word lamb, women, or trees. It could cover the tongue, health, death or an emotion. In general, we cover more sections of the Bible in a Topical study because the things we want to study (topical vs. typological) can be found in more places within the Bible. I say generally because most of the time typology is related to specific instances instead of a broad view of a subject.

Similar to Typology, we use concordance to find the subject matter we are looking for. In some cases, we might look up the word "lamb" and find that some of the events do not correspond with the type of lamb stories we want. If we are looking for only lambs used in sacrificial settings, we

---

[6] Not everything is an allegory or similar. Be careful to check out any theories to see if other Bible scholars have noted what you did. If none have, then look closer to see that you don't stretch the text out of shape in making your point. Better to not say something that could be right than to say something that is wrong.

would have to discard lambs use as part of a flock. Therefore, we can narrow down our verses by looking at the extra words of the concordance, sometimes we will have to go to the Bible to see if the verse is about sacrificing or eating.

Topical Concordance Example

Taking water as an example, focused on the spiritual and not the literal, and with an understanding that many examples will arise, I will assign members of the study to different places in the Bible to look up verses. They are given instructions to prioritize them with only spiritual meanings being used for the study.

Below is a portion of a concordance for NIV:

> "Sir," the woman said, "you have nothing to draw with and the well is deep. Where can you get this living water?"
> (NIV John 4:11)

> "Jesus answered, "Everyone who drinks this water will be thirsty again,"
> (NIV John 4:13)

> "but whoever drinks the water I give them will never thirst. Indeed, the water I give them will become in them a spring of water welling up to eternal life."
> (NIV John 4:14)

> "The woman said to him, "Sir, give me this water so that I won't get thirsty and have to keep coming here to draw water."
> (NIV John 4:15)

> "Then, leaving her water jar, the woman went back to the town and said to the people,"
> (NIV John 4:28)

> "Once more he visited Cana in Galilee, where he had turned the water into wine. And there was a certain royal official whose son lay sick at Capernaum."
> (NIV John 4:46)

> **"Sir," the invalid replied, "I have no one to help me into the pool when the water is stirred. While I am trying to get in, someone else goes down ahead of me."**
> **(NIV John 5:17)**

You can see as you read through a portion of the page, some are physical water and some are spiritual depending on the verse. In a word study on spiritual water, you would have to discard those scriptures that were literally physical water.

In doing a topical study, the leader has to be more flexible in listening and interpreting the meaning of different passages until a complete picture is achieved. It is like a hologram. A hologram is possible by using many facets of the same picture using lasers. If one of the laser beams is not working properly you still get the picture but it is not as clear. Each laser beam layers upon the others to give a clearer picture. The same thing applies to the information in the Bible.

In the list, John 4:15 shows the woman is thinking that Jesus means literal water, however we may want that included in our lesson as it shows the contrast between spiritual water and what the woman thought it was. This brings up a needed point: When a person is confused about whether to include a verse, always include it. It gives the class something to talk about and helps them learn what to include or not to include in these types of studies.

So, in the Bible we start with a singular idea or fact. By doing a topical study, we draw on more scriptures to see more facets of the same subject. We quickly learn we need more information. Therefore, we followed the thread of words to determine what was being said.

Finding Answers in the Word of God

We have a great example of God preparing the pages of the Old Testament to agree with the New Testament and get that right answer by a word study (Topical study). There are things that come together as we do a book study and there are things that come together when we do a topical or typological study. All of the studies are great. The idea is that we want to use the Bible to inform people about the Father, Son and Holy Spirit.

These studies give us a variety of ways to teach people about God. People get bored doing the same kind of study week after week. In addition, you, as the teacher, get to use your ability as an "Ambassador for God."

**"We are therefore Christ's ambassadors, as though God were making his appeal through us. We implore you on Christ's behalf: be reconciled to God."
(NIV 2nd Co 5:20)**

**"Now then we are ambassadors for Christ, as though God did beseech you by us: we pray you in Christ's stead, be ye reconciled to God."
(KJV 2nd Co 5:20)**

When we teach we have the most important job in the universe, bringing people to God. As ambassadors, we come from a different place than all others. We get the privilege to share information about eternity and a Savior. But, it is so important you may feel inadequate. We all are. However, the Bible is not.

When we teach we are using the tools God has given us. In the Bible, we have an enormous amount of subjects and different ways to excite and educate people. Never think you are alone. The Holy Spirit is right there showing you and directing your class. If you sincerely desire to glorify God, He will teach you.

A topical study could be on how God eases grief or death or helps us out of depression or marital problems. These are important everyday topics that mean so much to people.

There are topological and similar studies that teach about being obedient to God and having faith and trust in Him. This is important for people feeling angry, put upon or alone.

There is an inexhaustible amount of situations that these types of studies cover.

The lessons discussed in this chapter are written to help you in your quest. They prove that the Bible is different and must have been inspired by God. Not every lesson will excite everyone. Sometimes it really speaks to a few sometimes only one. However, over the course of using these different things, you will excite everyone and you will encourage everyone. Always know that every time you teach, God loves you and listens to your class. If you were only teaching and trying for Him alone, it is enough.

Chapter X

"Do not conform to the pattern of this world, but be transformed by the renewing of your mind. Then you will be able to test and approve what God's will is— his good, pleasing and perfect will."
(NIV Rom 12:2)

Application of Bible Principles for Everyday Life

I never realized what coming to the Lord meant until I decided that I needed Jesus in my life. I grew up in a Presbyterian church and my mother was the superintendent of the Sunday school portion of the Sunday services. Of course, I had to go and participate. As I grew up, I went through all the classes and became a part of the adult church. However, when I got to be about 18 years old, I decided that organized religion was not for me and I left the church.

It always seemed like something was missing in my life. I had been searching for years to find out what life was all about. When I was 42 years old, I decided I should give the Bible one more look. After exhaustive study, I came to the Lord and I discovered what being born again really meant. My mind looked at things differently. I cannot explain when or how it happened, but I looked at everything differently. It was similar to one day I liked chocolate ice cream and now I like vanilla (It could be vice versa).

My taste and attitude toward life changed. I found out what renewing my mind literally means. What a wonderful journey it was. Now, my mind is renewed every time I study the Bible. I build my faith, add to my knowledge of God and His Word, and I feel energized and renewed in my spirit as well. It is why studying the Bible is so important to me. It is why implementing and applying Bible principles in my life is a goal I strive for every day. It is also where I get the energy and knowledge to lead Bible studies with strangers, friends, and family.

-Brent Mackey

One of the most used methods of studying the Bible is learning how to apply its principles to ever day life. As such, understand that Scripture cannot be separated from learning how to apply it. It is interesting that the Jewish word Torah means the "Law." However, it is not a law as we understand the term. It is much more. It is a law that teaches.

If a child is reaching for a hot pan and the parent says never touch it or you'll get burned and proceeds to show the child what happens to things that touch something hot, we have a learning/teaching law. If a child obeys the law of not touching hot things, the reward is not getting burnt. If a Jewish person reads the Old Testament, it's the same kind of thing; the readers should want to put into practice what they read. The Law was written to teach. Without applying it in everyday life, we would miss using the purpose for which God inspired the Bible to be written.

Putting Faith into Practice

Today when the Bible is read and taught, we sometimes get caught up in the "theology" of it all. Answering questions like, "Are other denominations better than the one we have chosen;" Or "What are the differences between churches?" By picking apart details that are argumentative, people miss gaining the general knowledge of how we should be putting our faith into practice.

To get the most out of studying the Bible we concentrate on application first before any other aspect of study, wherever possible. The Bible should make you think of sermons, meditations, and what things are needed to change in your life to be more like Christ.

The goal then as a Bible study leader is to motivate the student to take a journey. This trip is about realizing what God would want for his/her life. Below are verses that are Paul's responses when he heard about the Colossian believers having a strong desire for the Lord.

> **"For this reason, since the day we heard about you, we have not stopped praying for you and asking God to fill you with the knowledge of his will through all spiritual wisdom and understanding.**
> **And we pray this in order that you may live a life worthy of the Lord and may please him in every way: bearing fruit in every good work, growing in the knowledge of God,"**
> **(NIV Col 1:9, 10)**
>
> **"For this cause we also, since the day we heard it, do not cease to pray for you, and to desire that ye might be filled with the knowledge of his will in all wisdom and spiritual understanding;**

That ye might walk worthy of the Lord unto all pleasing, being fruitful in every good work, and increasing in the knowledge of God;"
(KJV Col 1:9, 10)

As you can see by the above verses, Paul considers prayer of upmost importance when talking about a teacher's attitude toward students and believers in the faith. His prayer includes filling them with knowledge of God's will for their lives. He also talks about growing in the knowledge of God.

When talking with students two things should be made abundantly clear:

First, they should gain knowledge of God through reading the Bible. It will tell them the types of things God likes and what He dislikes his people doing. It becomes evident through the various events that took place in the Bible. It also comes through in the Law given to Moses. Learning what the Bible says about how Jesus acted gives us insight on the applications of God's Word in our lives as Christians. The light of the New Testament shines on the Old Testament to give us understanding of how we should be as Christians today. It will give us insight on how to interpret the things in the Old Testament in light of Christ and His sacrifice on the cross.

The second thing is the motivation. It's not in the accomplishing works that pleases God as much as the motivation that is in our hearts. When we love the Lord, we strive hard to please and glorify Him. The way that we do that is by taking His Word and applying it in our lives out of love for Him. He showed us His love for us on the cross. Our faith is generated by that love.

"We love because he first loved us."
(NIV 1st John 4:19)

"We love him, because he first loved us."
(KJV 1st John 4:19)

Certainly, the Holy Spirit takes those things that are of Christ and gives us spiritual wisdom and growth in knowledge. But, motivation will answer a plethora of questions. For example, "I strive hard to do what God wants me to do but sometimes I can't get it right. Is God going to hate me?" My answer is that "it is the striving to do the right thing that pleases God". No one gets it right or is perfect all the time. If your motivation is to glorify God in your actions (Without ulterior motives) this will please God. Even if you get it a little wrong once in a while or are unsuccessful in your attempt. Then I go on to explain God is not a God of hate, but of love.

Everyone Can Get Involved

In giving lessons, it is important that the leader key on points that may be harder for people to remember, especially if the points are essential to understanding our faith.

This "question and answer" technique will get everyone involved with the study. Picking up and expanding on Bible ideas can get boring. At first glance, the individual points seem self-explanatory. However, there is a way that we as teachers can help our students own the ideas. Owning an idea means the point that is being made becomes clear and internalized. The person that gets caught up in the ideas of the study and takes a journey with the leader will start to put him or herself into that situation. A person will no longer be seeing it objectively, and in a sense coldly, without connection to the principle being discussed but will understand it up close and personal.

Car salespeople are told to put potential buyers in the driver's seat. Let them smell that new car odor, feel the comfort of the car seats, and experience the new car's drivability. This is done to make the person know how it would feel if they owned the vehicle themselves.

That in a very real sense is exactly what we want to do in a Bible study. Let the student take that journey in their minds. By asking questions, they will think in terms of what they are already doing and what they should do differently. Just like the test drive, people have an opportunity to experience the feelings of incorporating Bible principles in their own lives. Since everyone is experiencing the questions and answers, even if it is by others, everyone will hopefully internalize the feelings as their own. A teacher teaches best when people get involved to that degree.

An Example

Application study can take several ways to make class different and enjoyable. For example, role-playing is an excellent way to add something to your class. Name a situation that is upsetting like two people arguing about an everyday subject. Let's take road rage for example. Two men in a heated discussion, one is a truck driver and the other a driver of a car. The truck swerved into the lane of the car and the driver in the car blew his hor. At which time the truck driver had to break and get back in his lane or get hit. You pick two people to be the drivers. Have each explain why they are upset.

Car driver's reasons for being so upset (Perhaps):
1. He is going to make me late for work.
2. He could have hurt me badly.
3. He could have damaged my new car.
4. He should not have done what he did.
5. He made my life pass before my eyes.
6. He must be an idiot or blind.

Truck driver's reasons for being upset (Perhaps):
1. He was driving too fast.
2. He came up behind me and stayed in my blind side.
3. He should have known I would be turning I had on my signal.
4. He should know to be careful around a truck after all I would have destroyed his car.
5. He should know I'm on a strict schedule and he will cause me to be delayed.
6. He must be stupid or just a troublemaker.

Now the class gets to discuss any other reasons why either driver was correct in what was being said. You could ask who they felt was in the wrong. Also, any other reasons this occurred. After people get a chance to add a few things the leader announces as we are studying Luke chapter 6 our application lesson for tonight is Luke 6:31:

"Do to others as you would have them do to you."
(NIV Luke 6:31)

"And as you wish that others would do to you, do so to them."
(KJV Luke 6:31)

So, the question for discussion is, what should have happened in this situation? What do you think would have changed if they were Christians trying to live by the Golden rule? There's a saying that "angry people are seldom reasonable and reasonable people are seldom angry". It certainly goes along with the golden rule idea.

After that discussion say: let's look at a few other verses that give more meaning as well as a way to help us do the right thing in these types of situations. Look at the King James Version as it expands on the meaning. Ask how the class feels these verses should have applied to the situation.

> **"But I tell you, love your enemies and pray for those who persecute you,"**
> **(NIV Matt 5:44)**

> **"But I say unto you, Love your enemies, bless them that curse you, do good to them that hate you, and pray for them which despitefully use you, and persecute you;"**
> **(KJV Matt 5:44)**

And what about:

> **"A gentle answer turns away wrath,"**
> **(Prov 15:1)**

> **"A soft answer turneth away wrath: but grievous words stir up anger."**
> **(Prov 15:1)**

Before becoming a Christian this exact incident with the car and the truck happened to me. I was driving the car. He got out of his truck and I got out of my car. But, he said something that I hadn't considered. He had his signal on to turn right and I paid very little attention to it other than he was turning. When he came out of his truck, he said, "I'm not a car I have to go in the other lane to take a turn, this is an 18 wheeler you know! Now I have to go all the way around – way out of my way to turn around to make this turn again." He was right I was wrong even though it was out of ignorance. I was mad and he was mad, but when he said that I immediately got in my car and left.

In hindsight, I wish I had apologized and helped him back the truck up so it would have saved him time. But, that is what the Lord would have wanted me to do and I wasn't a Christian at the time, I didn't know Him. Knowing what I do now and looking back on it, I feel bad about what happened.

Use what you know and apply it to a Bible teaching. It doesn't have to be something you experienced personally every time. You can borrow incidents. But, by using real events, it becomes relevant to everyone. The way you present it, state it and are able to picture the event in your mind gives an excitement of authenticity.

The lesson now becomes a part of the student's mind because they've taken that journey. They've been involved with the feelings of both people.

They've put themselves in the situation and they have a practical experience they will remember. They not only drove the new car but they own it now too. Bible application studies build one upon another. The Word of God changes us into people that are better than they would have been without it (Not better than anyone else)

When students start applying what the Bible talks about in their everyday life, they feel better about themselves. Not in a conceited way, but in a cleaner way within themselves. They feel the rightness of what they do. They also begin to hate it when they fall short (Everyone falls short). The Holy Spirit convicts us when we sin and leads us to understand and apply the studies to our lives.

There are many other ideas for applying Biblical principles. Role-playing is a good one, but at the very least when discussing these things give the people a chance to interact with the ideas and even tell stories of their own. It's in the interaction that people will relate to a principle. Reading it in the Bible is useless if people can't solidify new concepts in a way they will remember and feel good about it. They need to see themselves after the change in their attitude and motivation. They need to remember that there was a time when they should have done things differently.

This formula of asking questions is an excellent way to discuss applying God's word in the students' lives. The more you build each of these chapters upon with the next, the greater vision you will have for Bible studies and the more confident you will become.

Chapter XI

> "And beginning with Moses and all the Prophets, he explained to them what was said in all the Scriptures concerning himself."
> (NIV Luke 24:27)

Building Peoples Faith

When people read the Bible, they will always find things that, like carving out a new revelation, really make them think. These areas of interest are what I call hot buttons, and it always amazes me how many hot buttons people have. You can see them at every Bible study. It's when a person starts to talk about a subject or asks a question. The more a person asks questions or talks about a subject the more interest they have and the greater is the intensity of their passion.

Correlating an idea is interesting for people at first, but somewhere along the way, after things line up in the Bible, enough correlations are made to make a head/heart connection. When that happens, people realize the Bible is much more than just another good book. It must be truly inspired by God. There is no other answer.

When students conclude the only answer is God, faith is built. Correlating the different facets of the Bible is one way that people will eventually come to know the truth.
-Brent Mackey

As Bible studies leaders, we have many topics to teach, but the most important effort we undertake is opening the student's hearts to the Holy Spirit. Correlating is a major tool that can achieve this. Through the study of events that relate to one another the student can first realize that God exists. Then they realize He transcends time and knows the end from the beginning. Finally, they come to understand that He plans ahead for events that occur. That's a tall order and one that shows there is a God.

Thankfully, God has given us many correlations throughout the Bible. One is through predictions and another is through the mentioning of scientific facts. Through the progression of your Bible studies, the unveiling of these connections will lead students to the moments that bring them closer to God.

Correlating Over the Centuries

The Bible has so many examples of how awesome God is. Linking ideas with historical events found in the New Testament with predictions from the Old Testament is one of the best ways.

In Genesis, for example, there is a figure that comes on the scene in chapter 14. The set up for this passage is that Lot had been taken away by an enemy, along with many people and goods. Abram (Later became Abraham) went with his men and some others and rescued the people and goods as well as the spoils from the enemy. The event is recorded from that point:

> "He recovered all the goods and brought back his
> relative Lot and his possessions, together with the
> women and the other people.
> After Abram returned from defeating Kedorlaomer
> and the kings allied with him, the king of Sodom
> came out to meet him in the Valley of Shaveh (that
> is, the King's Valley).
> Then Melchizedek king of Salem brought out bread
> and wine. He was priest of God Most High, 19 and
> he blessed Abram, saying,
> "Blessed be Abram by God Most High,
> Creator of heaven and earth.
> And praise be to God Most High,
> who delivered your enemies into your hand."
> Then Abram gave him a tenth of everything."
> (NIV Gen 14:16-20)

> "And he brought back all the goods, and also
> brought again his brother Lot, and his goods, and
> the women also, and the people.
> And the king of Sodom went out to meet him after
> his return from the slaughter of Chedorlaomer, and
> of the kings that were with him, at the valley of
> Shaveh, which is the king's dale.
> And Melchizedek king of Salem brought forth bread
> and wine: and he was the priest of the most high
> God.
> And he blessed him, and said, Blessed be Abram of
> the most high God, possessor of heaven and earth:

And blessed be the most high God, which hath
delivered thine enemies into thy hand. And he gave
him tithes of all."
(KJV Gen 14:16-20)

The only other time that Melchizedek is mentioned in the Old
Testament is in Psalms 110:

"The LORD has sworn
and will not change his mind:
"You are a priest forever,
in the order of Melchizedek."
(NIV Psalm110:4)

The LORD hath sworn, and will not repent, Thou art
a priest for ever after the order of Melchizedek."
(KJV Psalm 110:4)

When we read in the New Testament book of Hebrews, the writer
makes a case for Jesus being able to serve as a priest even though He is
from the tribe of Judah. The Levites coming from the tribe of Levi were
to be the priestly tribe. Judah was the royal or kingly tribe. As such, Jesus
being a king doesn't go against the Jewish Law however Jesus being a priest
does go against what the Jewish people believed. At that time, all priests
came from the priestly tribe of Levi.

Jesus would have been breaking the Law had not Melchizedek come
into play. In Hebrews, chapters 6 and 7, the writer relies on the Old
Testament Psalm written by David to say that Jesus has a right to be priest
by the order of Melchizedek.

The questions that come to mind are, why did David write the verse in
the psalm about Melchizedek or even remember the small section of
scripture written in Genesis. How did David know another would come
by that order, instead of the normal way of being a Levite? A vary minor
amount of information is given about this person and yet it's enough to
validate Jesus being priest and king. Jesus was also prophet proven by what
He said and did.

In teaching events, we as leaders need to be sensitive to these minor
details that pack a knockout punch when talking about the inspiration of
God in the Bible. There are many instances in the Bible just like this
example.

Correlating Through Science

Correlation also happens when we use the knowledge contained in the Bible that mentions a scientific fact. We know it is a fact because of the knowledge we have today but no one would have known at the time the Bible was written. It then becomes apparent that God inspired the writers to include information they actually did not know. In our teaching, it is important to build faith by showing examples of God's knowledge and foreknowledge wherever possible. Knowledge that should not be known by the author writing the book or knowledge of exactly what we humans need to know to get through life's problems is seen in prophecy (telling about things before they happen).

As an example, here is what the Bible says about how many stars are in the sky.

**"He took him outside and said, 'Look up at the sky and count the stars—if indeed you can count them.' Then he said to him, 'So shall your offspring[a] be.'"
(NIV Gen 15:5)**

**"And he brought him forth abroad, and said, Look now toward heaven, and tell the stars, if thou be able to number them: and he said unto him, So shall thy seed be."
(KJV Gen 15:5)**

**"I will surely bless you and make your descendants as numerous as the stars in the sky and as the sand on the seashore. Your descendants will take possession of the cities of their enemies,"
(NIV Gen 22:17)**

**"That in blessing I will bless thee, and in multiplying I will multiply thy seed as the stars of the heaven, and as the sand which is upon the sea shore; and thy seed shall possess the gate of his enemies;"
(KJV Gen 22:17)**

"I will make the descendants of David my servant and the Levites who minister before me as countless

as the stars in the sky and as measureless as the sand
on the seashore."
(NIV Jer 33:22)

"As the host of heaven cannot be numbered, neither
the sand of the sea measured: so will I multiply the
seed of David my servant, and the Levites that
minister unto me."
(KJV Jer 33:22)

This for us today is not a remarkable notion. However, knowing when these statements were written makes it extremely remarkable. Genesis was written approximately 1450 years BC and Jeremiah was written between 590 and 630 BC. As we read in the verses, the stars are not able to be counted. However, one of the first people to count the stars was Hipparchus between 160 and 130 BC approximately. The first star catalogue of his contained between 1025 and 1080 stars. The next catalogue came out approximately 100 AD. That would be about 700 years after Jeremiah was written. Totally disregarding the Bible, it was determined that there were 1022 stars. Ptolemy did this in his work called "Almagest".

Another counting of the stars was by a man named Ali-Kudsi; he produced a catalogue of stars listing the number at 992 published in 1437. Tycho Brahe produced a catalogue in 1598 that listed the stars at 965.

We of course, know there are billions upon billions of stars in the Milky Way galaxy alone. Since the telescope was invented in the 17th century, the astronomers have come to know that the stars can't be counted. There are far too many. But, the Bible accurately tells us that the stars are too numerous to count, like the sand on the seashore. Long before it was proven true. Who could have inspired that to be written at the time it was? Only one conclusion, it had to be God.

This correlation needs to be brought up during a Bible study because the average person doesn't make the connection. They know it to be true, so thinking about the time period that it was written is not on their radar. Nevertheless, it certainly helps to build confidence and a basis to believe the Bible was inspired by God. It becomes a building block for their faith.

Is it Coincidence?

When we look at the inspiration of God in the Scriptures, someone may want to explain away some bit of foreknowledge or prophecy. They may claim coincidence or some other way of looking at the incident being illustrated. We have to say that the inspiration of God is proven by the vast amount of coincidences, similarities, typology and outright prophecies. A particular passage may be taken two ways and thus may not be as concrete an example of foreknowledge as another may. But, the possibility exists that it IS foreknowledge. As coincidence will rear its ugly head as a possibility, don't be unduly concerned. Agree that another explanation is a possibility.

However, that line of reasoning starts to lose power as the amount of so-called "coincidences" begins to grow. One coincidence can be explained away but, what about 100 coincidences or 300 coincidences and more. Eventually it becomes very apparent that although some "coincidences" can be explained away, the sheer amount of them begs the answer that God inspired the Bible to be written.

Biblical Examples

For some people the examples below may seem to be coincidences. Taken individually we can understand why it appears this way. However, when we put them together they become a fulfilled prophecy.

The New Testament talks about the wise men asking where Jesus is being born is a coincidence in that the King tells them he will be born in Bethlehem:

> "'But you, Bethlehem, in the land of Judah, are by no means least among the rulers of Judah; for out of you will come a ruler who will shepherd my people Israel.'"
> (NIV Matt 2:6)

> "And thou Bethlehem, in the land of Juda, art not the least among the princes of Juda: for out of thee shall come a Governor, that shall rule my people Israel."
> (KJV Mat 2:6)

Old Testament (Micah was active in 722 BC) correlation:
> "But you, Bethlehem Ephrathah, though you are small among the clans[a] of Judah, out of you will come for me one who will be ruler over Israel, whose origins are from of old, from ancient times."
> (NIV Micah 5:2)

> "But thou, Bethlehem Ephratah, though thou be
> little among the thousands of Judah, yet out of thee
> shall he come forth unto me that is to be ruler in
> Israel; whose goings forth have been from of old,
> from everlasting."
> (KJV Micah 5:2)

As you notice in the above, the Old Testament verse, the ruler of Israel will be from everlasting. Only one person could be from everlasting that would be God.

Another very interesting scripture out of the Old Testament comes into play as far as the Son of God being God. We use it every Christmas without realizing, it was written by Isaiah about 740 BC.

> "For to us a child is born,
> to us a son is given,
> and the government will be on his shoulders.
> And he will be called
> Wonderful Counselor, Mighty God,
> Everlasting Father, Prince of Peace."
> (NIV Isaiah 9:6)

So the son is going to be called the Father, Mighty God, Wonderful counselor and Prince of Peace. How is that possible? Let's look at a New Testament corresponding passage:

> "Therefore go and make disciples of all nations,
> baptizing them in the name of the Father and of the
> Son and of the Holy Spirit,"
> (NIV Matt 28:19)

> "Go ye therefore, and teach all nations, baptizing
> them in the name of the Father, and of the Son, and
> of the Holy Ghost:"
> (KJV Matt 28:19)

Notice that in Matthew 28:19 all three parts of the trinity are included. Now notice that the word name is singular. Why? We know that God wants us to think of Him as one, three parts but all one God. Can you see the consistency throughout the Bible? This is just the tip of the iceberg. There are numerous correlations throughout the Bible like this.

So, although a coincidence can always be claimed, upon closer inspection the idea of coincidences starts to fade, and the clearer picture of inspiration seems a certainty. And again, as the tremendous amounts of these incidences occur the idea of the super naturalness of the Bible becomes a reality. Bible teaching and correlation to inspiration whenever possible will reinforce this reality because inspirations of God are clearly seen. Remember, the Holy Spirit is always active enabling people to see more clearly and opening the heart for reception.

We Need to be Patient

Now, the hardest part of teaching is that some people need to have preconceived ideas challenged by the Bible before they can start to learn. We need to show unbelievers more and more correlating information before they can let go of ideas they've held for a long time. If we openly disagree with a new person's premise and say they are wrong, they may stop coming to class. So, we can allow ourselves to lose the battle win the war. We cannot say they're right, but we do not have to be dogmatic about the facts that we believe are clearly in the Bible. We must continually allow room for doubt until the overwhelming truth becomes evident. It is one of the hardest things to do as a teacher.

I've listed only a few examples of how correlating these Biblical facts will help people to learn more and build their faith. But, over a period of time, you will see people change before your eyes. As their faith grows, so does their commitment to the Lord. He becomes more real and clearer in every facet of their faith. Every time we talk about Jesus the impact becomes greater and greater as their faith has been built up to accept the Bible as the Word of God. That means the gospel message about Jesus is true and reliable. It begins to bring everything together to a wonderful unshakeable faith.

Do you see why showing the awesomeness of God in teaching foreknowledge and prophecy are so important? It is because, once people realize in their hearts, not just their heads through the awesomeness of foreknowledge and prophecy, that God really exists and has written the Bible for us because He loves us, the Bible comes alive. The very words of the Bible start to mean greater things. The ideas and promises start being depended upon, because people see the awesomeness of God's inspiration contained in the Bible. The Holy Spirit is a wonderful teacher, but for whatever reason God wants us involved with the process. Therefore, we work hard learning the best way for us to teach and get points across to people and let the Holy Spirit do the rest. We are only responsible to try our best. Then we need not worry about the outcome afterward, that's up to God.

Chapter XII

"Be diligent in these matters; give yourself wholly to them, so that everyone may see your progress. Watch your life and doctrine closely. Persevere in them, because if you do, you will save both yourself and your hearers."
(NIV 1 Timothy 4:15, 16)

Baring Your Heart for the Lord

There is somewhat of a surprise, especially for men, when they come to the Lord. There are changes. The first change that most men tell me is that they no longer want to use the Lord's name in vain. It is the first thing they feel convicted about. Other things come along as the Holy Spirit helps people recognize ways that they should improve their walk with the Lord. But, the one surprise that is unexpected is heightened compassion. Christian men have told me that they even cry at some television commercials.

I confess, I have cried at commercials too. Things that never bothered me that way started bothering me. I feel for people in a much bigger way. But, we men do not like to show that side of us. For some reason we feel it makes us weaker. But, this change empowers us to do the things God would want us to do. Let people see our heart in an open way because of our love for them. It is not easy for men to do that. However, God surprises us with gifts we need to enable us to do a proper job for Him.

Preparing students for ideas and teaching moments can be so rewarding. For instance, an interesting thing happens when you tell people things about verses and about the Lord that touched your very heart. Their attention is focused, and interest is peaked. Something that impacts your soul may do the exact same thing for theirs. It could be that, for those moments when you can honestly relive your first experience of reading a section, you take your students along for the ride. They feel your excitement and they are impacted by it. Your honesty and exposed heart make a big difference.

-Brent Mackey

No Faking

This technique (Baring your heart) is to be used only when it is true. Don't ever pretend or "fake it" with your students. It just doesn't work well and it's not what the Lord would want. In other words, never do anything just for effect.

Preparing students in this way can be overused – so use it wisely and discriminately. Share ideas in that way and it will ring true because you are being true. It is so much more effective when people sense you are divulging your inner feelings. So, do not be afraid, loosen up and tell it from the heart.

It Makes Things More Interesting

I told a men's group that a certain set of verses (Or a story) in the Bible made me feel happy and uplifted. Then I proceeded to read the part that did that. The group's attention span was greater than most other times because I told them what it did for me prior to reading it. Bible ideas become much more memorable because students take a little trip in their minds trying to understand why it was so impacting on the leader or anyone else in the study for that matter.

Our minds are wonderful things – we really do want to learn subjects of interest to us. We also want to understand how we can feel good or happy like someone else. So because I prepared the scripture reading the way I did, they were prepared to feel happy and to understand why I was happy reading the passage. They all admitted having a more impacting response about the same Scripture even if they read it many times before. This response happens with other emotions as well.

Mentioning a personal heartfelt experience will add spice to the Bible study. Also, if an emotion is being discussed and you feel like telling the class about a Scripture that elicited that response in you, share it with the class.

Sometimes the experiences and emotions are so intimate that it may be hard to discuss them with your Bible Study. However, because it is so rewarding to explain some of your own feelings to the group where it applies to scripture, I would suggest that you try a little at a time until you reach a place at which you still feel comfortable.

Also, make sure you are not making others in the room feel uncomfortable. The object is to help students learn more about the Lord not necessarily more about you as the leader. As long as your focus is right, give it a try. See if it works well for your group.

Peaking People's Interest

To give a good, memorable Bible study it is important to hit on as many points that will impact people in the study as possible. People are moved if they are being educated and can feel growth. The way people get excited is if they have a good time, people get impacted if they are meeting friends and/or feel part of a group and if they are touched emotionally. It also intrigues people if something is unique or unusual.

Telling stories and baring you soul/heart to others is one of those ways. You can do the same thing if you tell a story about someone else baring his or her heart. This time though you can use that experience in two ways:

1. You can tell a story about how someone bared his or her heart and say that you felt that it was not a good thing to do and that you wouldn't have done that. Then follow up with "What do you think?" In this way it can become a conversation starter and you can talk about feelings and the best way to handle them.

2. You can tell a story and preface it by saying that the person was very courageous to bare his or her heart in the way they did and ask them if they would have done it.

The reason this is effective is because it will give a short break from the Bible study itself, and it allows new people, that may or may not have been joining in, to have a chance too. You see, everyone can have an opinion on this particular topic, whether they know the Bible well or not. It's more about human nature and feelings. It also builds relationships within the group. However, we don't want to get overly involved with personal issues or take it further than friendly advice. If you feel a person needs help, suggest a professional be consulted, your pastor or someone that can counsel them. At that point, it would be time to get back to the study.

Bible studies are better and more interesting if different things are included in them. Just remember the major focus in a Bible study is the Bible itself. However, we can always take a slight trip to change the mood. At the end of the night we want people to go home thinking about what they learned at the Bible study.

Chapter XIII

"And God has placed in the church first of all
apostles, second prophets, third teachers, then
miracles, then gifts of healing, of helping, of
guidance, and of different kinds of tongues. Are all
apostles? Are all prophets? Are all teachers? Do all
work miracles?"
(NIV 1Cor 12:28, 29)

Fulfilling Expectations – Tips

I used to think that anyone who understood the Bible would be able to teach it. This idea was based on the notion that teaching was about knowing facts. My attitude changed when I started teaching others. I found that standing in front of people and giving out all the wonderful things that interested me, did not excite others at all. I could not believe it at first. How was it that people were not experiencing the passion that I had experienced? I had taught classes previously, but the audience was learning how to do a job and getting paid to learn what I was saying. Not realizing the difference, I thought there must be something lacking in the people coming to the study. Then I noticed in 1 Corinthians chapter 12 that not everyone was appointed to be a teacher.

A retired preacher told me "You cannot do anything well without learning how to do it first." In other words, you do not know whether God has given you a gift unless you try to learn how to use it. That opened-up a world of possibilities. But, mainly I realized that when God gives you a talent it still requires you to learn the basics of subject (a method) it in order to be able to put that talent to a good use. That means that it takes time to learn how to teach. I realized that the people who attend have some impact on the dynamics in the class, but it has a lot to do with the way the teacher teaches.

Bible studies are voluntary and not the same as the teaching I had done in the past. So, I decided to learn about how to teach a Bible study in a way that motivates and excites people. I also learned that the style of teaching has to do with the personality of the teacher. All leaders are different and must adapt the teaching method they choose to their own teaching style.

The very first basic foundation of a Bible study is to realize what people expect and want from a study. These are the things we need to fulfill if we want to have a well-received study.

-Brent Mackey

Expectations

To understand how to motivate people it is important to understand what people expect out of a Bible study. Knowing these expectations will prepare you to lead while avoiding distractions. It will also allow the students to focus on what you are teaching.

Here is what is typically expected:

- A nice atmosphere of love and acceptance
- A nice personable leader
- They are expecting to be told something that they do not already know
- They are expecting to be taught about the Bible by using the Bible
- They hope for and expect refreshments
- They expect it to be in keeping with a certain level of knowledge that would be right for them
- A hope that they will fit in to the group
- They may be worried having to speak in front of others

In order to motivate people, we first look to fulfill these expectations, or at least be aware of them and be prepared to address them if they should arise. We will cover each expectation throughout this chapter, but it is most important for you to find your teaching style and learn how you will handle each scenario.

An Atmosphere of Love and Acceptance

Love and acceptance in a Bible study should start the first time a person comes to it. I like to seat the new person next to me or at least close to me. The idea in doing this is not only to get acquainted with them but also to find the best way to help accomplish this person's goals for learning the Bible. With a new person close by, it becomes easier to start to understand who they are, how they learn, and what they expect to get out of the study. It helps to see when you hit a nerve or when it is important to go a little easier and explain a little more in depth. If there is any small talk before the Bible study, you will be able to talk with the new person and gain some needed background concerning the amount of knowledge, or lack thereof, he or she has.

However, one of the most important reasons you should pay attention to newer people is that they need to feel the love you have for them in

Christ. They will feel it more and more as they realize that you genuinely care about them. Some people do not have anyone to tell them that they are cared about. As the teacher, each student is important, and it is part of your responsibility to let them know you care about their spiritual wellbeing. This is not something that you do by just saying words. It is something you are doing by noticing them and being involved with the student's feelings. Validation and encouragement of people's existence and worth are so important.[7]

When you begin your study with love and encouragement for each newcomer, you are setting the tone for the rest of the classes. The time spent together should be considered as one of love and encouragement. The students will know what to expect and will keep in line with that expectation.

A Nice Personable Leader

Doesn't that sound so old fashion? However, the truth is that people find strength in a leader that is always trying to be nice to people and concerned about others. That is exactly what they hope to find at the Bible study.

At one time, I loved playing pocket billiards and had the privilege of being close friends with Irving Crane, a 15 times world pocket billiards champion. I learned a tremendous amount by just watching him play. Others did too. When he was practicing at a pool hall people would come up to him and want to play with him. He would say, "Well you can rack the balls if you want to, but I'm practicing for a tournament and I won't give you a shot. If I miss you certainly can take your turn." The people would invariably rack the balls for him for about 45 minutes and then thank him for letting them watch him play. They would always say it was worth it just to learn some things while they watched. He was a fantastic player. People used to come from all over the country just to watch him practice and they would learn how to become better players.

What would you give to have a good example when you want to learn how to do something? Examples are invaluable. It is especially important

---

[7] Warning- When dealing with the opposite sex be careful not to cross the familiarity line with students. It is quite easy for a person to consider you more than a teacher. Hopefully in a co-ed class both you and your spouse (If you have one) will be present. Always refer intimate problems to the same sex member, a person who will be better able to handle the problems. If you find that you are being thought of in a more personal way than is appropriate, it's time to make certain by your actions and words that the person feels the lack of that type of intimate connection with you. Remember, if a student of the opposite sex needs to talk, always make it a meeting beyond reproach by having someone else come to the meeting- preferably your spouse or another person of the same sex as the person needing help. In most cases it would be better to suggest a meeting with your spouse, another member at church or in the study group (of the same sex) to talk with if possible. In that way you insure a safe and secure atmosphere for the person needing help.

to see someone who is walking the talk concerning Biblical principles. It is much easier to understand application principles we teach in our Bible studies when someone sees a person doing it by walking with the Lord daily. Just as many learned from watching Irving Crane, it is the same with people who come to the Lord and want to be more like Him. They watch more mature Christians and take ideas from what they see mature Christians do.

So, what does a mature Christian look like; the one people expect to meet at the Bible study? The answer is that they think a mature Christian is you – that is what people will see, won't they? The teacher is always going to be what a student thinks Christians are really like. Good or bad. The person will make a value judgment based on how you act. Hopefully, they see a person that emulates Jesus, and it motivates them to become more like the Lord. Therefore, it is the responsibility of the teacher to portray Christ properly – in the way the lord would want them to act all the time.

> **"But the fruit of the Spirit is love, joy, peace, patience, kindness, goodness, faithfulness, 23 gentleness and self-control. Against such things there is no law."**
> **(NIV Gal 5:22, 23)**

> **"But the fruit of the Spirit is love, joy, peace, longsuffering, gentleness, goodness, faith, Gal 5:23 Meekness, temperance: against such there is no law."**
> **(KJV Gal 5:22, 23)**

If you have joy of the Lord it would mean that, for the most part, you are a happy person inside. You need to show it. If you have peace through Jesus and knowing Him, you should be exhibiting a quiet confidence in your conversation and in the way you act. If you are patient, it will be seen by others and admired. In addition, kindness to others is so important in showing Christ in you. Being careful of other's feelings and making people feel at ease showing gentleness and kindness, always salting your speech and action with love and goodness. These are the things that people expect and notice.

This type of attitude needs to be a part of your whole being. Do not act one way at Bible study, go out and act differently at other times. If you do act differently, people will see you and you will be giving them a good excuse to say derogatory things about Christianity. Remember in the 23rd

Psalm it says: "He leads us in the paths of righteousness for His name sake". The Holy Spirit will convict us because we wear our Savior's name. Therefore, we all know what goodness is and how we should act. If you are having a problem with trying (We can't always be perfect) to do that, then you should wait until you get that issue settled in your own mind before you become a teacher.

In conclusion, do your best to always exhibit the fruits of the Spirit. Seeing your close walk with the Lord, People will desire to have it for their own. Then, you will be that right example and your Bible study will grow, and you will see your students mature as well.

Expecting to Be Told Something They Do Not Know

This is a tall order, which should keep teachers humble. It is in humility that teachers learn more and more about a subject. Never thinking they know all the answers, will compel them to stretch themselves to research thoroughly the verse or subject being discussed. In that way, even if the lesson is short it can be expanded very easily when questions arise. Also, teachers should prefer to be able to answer questions when asked without coming back or revisiting the question the following week, if possible. This thinking and preparedness is exactly what teachers need to do to satisfy the more mature Christians' quests for knowledge. Do not let the fundamental truths and in-your-face answers become boring, treat each question as new and exciting.

They Are Expecting to Be Taught by Using the Bible

I have a pet peeve about some Bible study teachers. They often use other books, slides, and other sources for their Bible studies without consulting the Bible at all. I have seen so called Bible studies that are based on secular books one right after the other and calling it a Bible study.

A Bible study uses the Bible. I realize that some may think that it is a novel idea, but people come to a Bible study, I hope, to learn about the Bible. When people are not learning about the Bible, why not call the study a Christian book club or something similar. There is absolutely nothing wrong with a book club. However, it is not really a Bible study without opening the Bible. People who come to a Bible study expect to open a Bible and learn about it.

Now, if we were studying the Old Testament about David and the Philistines it would be great to see a map to understand geographically where things were and are today. It is appropriate to use this kind of material, but never without some Biblical purpose. The Bible study must be enhanced by the extra material and not the other way round.

In other words, to learn about the Bible by looking at other extra Biblical material is great. But, to learn about the extra material and then throw in a Bible verse calling it a Bible study does not make it one.

They Hope and Expect Refreshments

Not to seem trivial but people do expect to have refreshments at a Bible study. Often it is what makes them come back the first few weeks. Thinking about a Bible study and remembering the good things that were served sometimes lessens the need for a super tremendous teacher.

Whether you assign the refreshments to different people each week or supply them yourself, try to have what people will like. I have found it is a great way to have new people want to come back. Hopefully, the feeling lasts until their faith is built to the point when they will not want to miss the study even if food is not offered.

We can take a lesson from Jesus. After Jesus fed the five thousand out of compassion, He knew they would come back, looking for food. Jesus said to the people, speaking in John:

> **"Jesus answered, "I tell you the truth you are looking for me, not because you saw miraculous signs but because you ate the loaves and had your fill."**
> **(NIV John 6:26)**

> **"Jesus answered them and said, Verily, verily, I say unto you, Ye seek me, not because ye saw the miracles, but because ye did eat of the loaves, and were filled."**
> **(KJV John 6:26)**

Our Lord certainly knows the heart of man and He knew that food would bring them back to see Him. So, He fed the five thousand and they did exactly that, they came to find Him. We can do the exact same thing when we give Bible studies in our homes. We can have the people enjoy themselves so much that when they think of a Bible study they also think of cookies and finger foods with plenty of coffee and sodas.

A great tip for Bible studies is to have snacks readily available throughout the study. That way people will not be wishing you would serve the cake half way into the study. Cake and things like that are great but there is something about being able to listen and eat at the same time that makes the study that much more enjoyable.

They Expect It to Be in Keeping with a Certain Level of Knowledge That Would Be Right for Them

One of the most rewarding things I experienced at a church service was a time when I was in my teens and it was the children's minute. This is when the preacher would ask all the children to come up front before being dismissed to their classroom. Their ages ranged from 5 years old to 8 years old.

I loved that time because the preacher made the message so simple that I could understand it. It may seem funny a 14 or 15-year-old boy liking a story for a 5-year-old. But, I could not help but love the simplicity of the message. As I grew older, I found that others had the same feeling as I did – and they were adults at the time it was being given to the children.

One stood out in my mind and I have never forgotten it. The preacher brought the children up front and presented them with an apple to inspect. It looked like a great apple the children agreed. Then the preacher brought out another apple that was all bruised on the outside and looked ugly. He again asked the children what they thought of that apple. Of course, they did not like that apple at all.

Then he cut both apples in half and took out one seed from each of the centers. He put them in the children's hands and asked them to look at them. They all said that they looked the same. To drive home his point, he further asked if anyone could tell which apple each of the seeds came from. By this time with all the passing around of the seeds none could tell or remember.

He then said that "each of you children have a spirit just the same as everyone else. They all look the same to God because, He looks on the inside and He loves them, no matter what they look like on the outside or what they have been through. Just like the apples have the same seed inside, we all are the same inside, and we need to love one another just like God loves all of us.

It was a simple lesson, but so memorable. People have an expectation of being able to understand what is going to be taught. Try to pinpoint the level of education you need to teach each class to make the class understandable to everyone. This will ensure that the class will fulfill the needs and expectations of everyone attending.

If you have a class that is filled with only mature Christians in it and a newer Christian comes in, talk with him about the level of difficulty that will be taught in the class. Suggest that you will either help him get up to speed, start a class for new believers or switch him to one that is already going on. You could also suggest giving him private Bible studies to begin with. At the very least, get him involved with a church Bible study, which is usually geared to all levels of Christian maturity and knowledge.

The points throughout this book are intended for general application, as is the point above. There are always exceptions to what is usual. The reason I make this observation is that I did have a class that was made up of Christian men that had over fifteen years of Bible studies and church classes under their belts. A newcomer wanted to come and be involved in the class anyway. Over the next 3 years, he mainly listened and asked questions about things he did not know. What a great class! He inspired everyone and today he has a tremendous knowledge of the Bible. Sometimes there are reasons for bending rules. So, do not be too dogmatic in your application of any suggestions. If there comes a time when an exception needs to be made, then make it.

Most of the classes that I teach are geared to all levels of knowledge so no one is left out. I do have some private studies that are attended by more knowledgeable students, but it would change if newer Christians started to attend.

The most important Bible study that can be given is to a new person not yet saved. Because it can result in being able to be used by God to help someone decide to follow Jesus. Evangelism takes precedent over any other type of Bible study. I will do my best to shuffle and re-schedule things to see a new person who wants to learn about the Lord.

However, in over 20 years I have only cancelled a pre-set appointment once because I was evangelizing. I do not think the Lord would want us to break appointments and commitments that have been already made to evangelize (I have been a few minutes late on several occasions though).

It is always important for people to see that Christians can be counted on to follow through with the personal commitments they make to other people. This obviously goes to our previous discussion on a leader being a good example.

They Hope They Will Fit In

This is one of the most pivotal points for every teacher to understand. People hope to fit in. We cannot teach people about the truth in the Lord if they are not going to stay in the study. How can you teach students who are not there? If people do not feel like they belong, they will not be back. Our chance to make a difference for the Lord is gone.

As I am writing this, a particular instance comes to mind where a newcomer did not attend past his second night. We were all just getting acquainted with him, but for some reason one of the men got talking about people living together. That night he went on for 15 to 20 minutes really driving his opinion home. The newcomer left that night and never came back. There are a lot of sins in the Bible, enough to go around any room several times. Although we often talk about Bible principles, we must be sensitive to each other.

It was a shame that he left. It would have been nice to have him there long enough for him to see the love of Christ and the faith we all have. The Holy Spirit has a great way of convicting people of anything they should be changing. Because he was living unmarried with a woman, he, of course, felt very much out of place. I do not condemn the fellow who went into a subject about living together, because at the time no one knew that the newcomer was doing that. However, it was a learning experience for all of us to realize if we want to impact people's lives it would be better for the Holy Spirit to do the convicting. Once we explain about God's word and the message of the saving grace of Jesus Christ, we should sit back and wait on the Spirit to move in a person's heart. Hammering an idea home concerning a particular sin (that may be a sore point with a new person) is not a good idea.

At the same time, we cannot rule out that the Holy Spirit may have urged the one in our group who, for seemingly no reason, got on the subject and belabored the point. Perhaps the newcomer needed to hear the facts exactly as they were given that night. But, I personally would try to err on the side of letting time pass before confronting a Christian living in any kind of sin. We also want to remember what Paul said in 1st Corinthians chapter 5 – that is - we are not to judge those outside the church. That applies to anyone coming to our study groups who are not Christians yet. When a person has time with a group and learns how much Christians love them and then become Christians, they are more willing to listen about shortcomings if they need to be brought up at all.

All this is to say that when a newcomer attends the Bible study it is important to make them feel like they are a welcome part of the group regardless of where they are in their walk. There will be time later to talk with him or her, should the need arise.

They are Worried About speaking

The number one fear, after death, is speaking in front of people. Of course, there are some that have no problem whatsoever with it, but most people are self-conscious. This is especially so in a new group or class. With unfamiliar faces all around the room staring at them it makes it hard for them. Later as the class progresses and the person knows the people in the group better, speaking-out is not such a daunting event.

There are some things that will ease the minds of a new class or a new person coming into a class. One is a survey for each member to fill out. Below are some sample questions that could be used. Please notice the tone of the question and how inoffensive the wording makes the question.

- Do you enjoy reading aloud, or prefer to listen as others read aloud?
- Do you mind being asked to participate, or would you rather participate at your own speed?
- Is praying aloud something you enjoy doing, or is listening to someone else pray more comforting to you?
- As I want everyone to get the fullest benefit from this class, would you say that you like to be called on to answer questions, or would prefer to answer questions by raising your hand?
- Note at the bottom: As time goes by please let me know if any of the above preferences change.

The reason for the survey is to make people feel comfortable and not anxious to come to class. I knew of a class that the leader insisted that everyone pray out loud. The teacher explained that it was important to the Christian growth of everyone in the class to participate. The next week the class was reduced by five members. So please be understanding of the fears of our weaker brothers and sisters in all different areas. Bible studies should be inclusive to everyone. Everyone needs them. Do not make people feel uncomfortable because you have not given enough time or understanding to another's weaknesses. Remember, because something does not bother you does not mean it cannot be a real obstacle for others.

These hints hopefully will encourage you to think a little more about the people that are attending your Bible study. Handled correctly it will be a wonderful and rewarding experience, not only for your guests/students but also for you.

Chapter XIV

"Consequently, faith comes from hearing the
message, and the message is heard through the word
about Christ."
(NIV Romans 10:17)

How to Start a Bible Study

*Starting Bible studies can be a daunting task. Especially if you think you have to
convince people to come to it. I started a prayer and accountability meeting with one other
person. He was a close friend and we felt it would help us in our walk with the Lord.*

*People like to know what's going on when you tell them you have a weekly meeting
at 8:00 in the morning. We only mentioned our meeting to a couple of people when we
started receiving calls asking to join us. I realized that there are plenty of people who
would like to go to a Bible study our prayer group.*

*Once you know that people want to come it seems much less daunting a task. People
are not rejecting you they are rejecting the idea of Bible studies. Usually when I'm with
a larger number of people I will only make the comment that I give Bible studies. Or I
may mention that I'm not free on a couple of days because I give Bible studies. This tells
them what I would like them to know without actually asking them to come to one.*

*I might also say to someone, when a large group is not present, that I give Bible
studies and follow up with the question "what do you think of the Bible?' Then I can
learn from their answer whether pursuing the idea of Bible study is even appropriate.*

*But one thing is certain I do not want to ever wonder if I should have gone further
talking with them about Bible study. Sometimes from their answers you can tell it would
be futile. But on the occasions when you don't know I would want to clarify what their
answer would be. In this case I risk to have no regrets.*

-Brent Mackey

First Things First

Having read this book to this point you should have a good idea about
giving Bible studies. But, where do you start?

Before going out to start teaching Bible studies, meet with your pastor
and ask him what he does when he meets with people for the first time.
Learn from him so you are on the same page as far as the information to
be given to new people. Bible studies outside of the church are a great way

to bring in new converts to Christ. Often people don't have a church and will come to yours. For that reason, it's important for you to become acquainted with exactly what your pastor feels is important for people to know. Working with him is essential for a seamless transition between an un-churched person and going to church for the first time.

Once you have spoken with your pastor and are comfortable with your initial approach with potential Bible study attendees, formulate your own initial Bible study using the information that you have gained through this book. Make your Bible studies comfortable and suitable for your overall abilities. Once that is done, you are ready to give a Bible study. All you need now is a willing class.

Your first study may be with friends or family members who are searching for a good study. That would be a comfortable place to start. Start slow and work out the kinks of getting your teaching style the way you want it. Obviously, let your class know that you are just starting out.

Begin with Bible subjects that you find fascinating. It's only natural that those are the ones that you will be more excited about. This is just the thing that makes people want to come to the Bible study. Excitement and enthusiasm are infectious. Friends will even ask you if they can come to your beginning Bible studies because of your passion.

They will be very forgiving and understanding. It doesn't matter how good you are to begin with. Part of my first Bible study was to ask my friends to help me make a list of what they wanted to discuss. Every week after that I prepared a class to cover one of those subjects. At the end of the night, we would discuss what we thought were the most important points. I made a list and gave it to them at our next Bible study. They learned a lot and I learned a lot more from every angle about giving my own Bible study.

When it comes to what to teach, refer to the "Formulating Bible Studies" chapter from earlier in this book. You are the leader, and as I stated before, what excites you may or may not excite your students. However, if it excites you then you will deliver a very enthusiastic Bible study. Begin with a topic that is right for you for your first study. There will be plenty of room to expand on topics for future studies.

The Next Bible Studies

With your first study group(s) behind you, there will be room to expand your network. The next group for me came from attendees that wanted me to go to other people's homes. This was extremely rewarding as it helped me to develop the best way for me (with my abilities and personality) to explain the Bible to people.

After honing your teaching skills, remember God draws people by working through others (teachers, evangelizers, etc.) that lead them to know Him. However, we would have to say that those who do Bible studies with unrelated people are hunters. We hunt for the lost. We may get people who are searching for someone or something and need our help to find a way to fill the void in their hearts. If we do not fill that void with the truth, they may be persuaded by others to believe a false path.

When the time comes to start fresh Bible studies, a teacher needs to become more pro-active, to go out and look for students to teach. This is also called evangelizing and witnessing. Obviously, you can be teaching in the church you go to. I have done that for the last 23 years. But, I am talking about independent Bible studies open to anyone from whatever church they are going to or for people that do not believe to begin with. This type of hunting is harder in terms of the possibility of being rejected. Nevertheless, you get used to it quickly and you may find that you are just right for that type of challenge. The more you try the better at it you become.

A friend of mine, who I met through church before he moved, is a pastor in a church 1500 miles away. One day I received a call from him, and he said, "My dad needs to go to a Bible study. I don't know whether he'll go or not, but could you give it a try. I know he would benefit from it." I knew his dad and he wasn't much for going to church, and he didn't know much about the Bible. I knew I would have to hit on an idea that would be hard for him to refuse. So, I arranged to see him and stopped by his house. After some small talk, I asked him if he wanted to come to a Bible study. He said, "Where is it?" I looked him in the eye, and I said, "At your house". He got a big grin on his face and said, "Why not, I'll be here anyway". That was over 10 years ago, and we still have Bible studies together. It's over the internet because of the Corona Virus situation, but we'll get back to meeting once that's over.

Another time I was at McDonalds and had struck up a conversation with a group of people. When the chance came, I introduced a few Biblical concepts that coincided with what was being talked about. We started talking about the Bible and one thing led to another and a Bible study convened the next day. We had it right where we were sitting. It resulted in three baptisms. That happened last year (2019) before the pandemic got going.

You cannot be in the right place at the right time unless you are available and out there trying. There is an old saying that goes something like this: "A Christian farmer prays for a good crop and says amen with a hoe". Don't pray for the Lord to bring people to you to teach and then stay at home waiting for God to bring someone to your door.

Dr. Livingstone, a missionary in Africa, was doing such wonderful work that articles were written about him in magazines. He had extended his practice far into the jungle. One of the Christian college professors wrote him a letter to offer him help. He wrote, "as soon as they build a road to where you are, we would like to have our students come and help you." Dr. Livingstone wrote back, "If they need a road don't send them".

Let's face facts; some people do not want to be hunters. They are more like farmers. A hunter loves to go out; there is an exhilaration in the hunt. A farmer gets exhilaration from watching things that have been planted grow. We need both. But, new Bible studies away from the church you go to is different. So, we need to be pioneers in a way. Every opportunity comes with a little anxiety or nervousness inside. However, it includes more rewards and experiences than you could ever get from anything else.

Refining Your Approach

To get started, introduce yourself to new people where you get coffee or go out for breakfast. Get involved with conversations there, if it is not intruding. I've watched others try to get things going but they don't realize that they are being obnoxious. Remember the Lord says we plant seeds. We do not jam them in the ground it would crush the seed itself. It's so much easier to just be nice about introducing the Bible or the Lord.

Have you ever told someone you had a secret? They will badger you about it, trying to make you tell them what it is. Curiosity is a real force. So, by being kind and biding your time with people, they will eventually want to talk about your subject (The Bible or the Lord). This is because your hints and your actions make them curious. You are not ramming it down their throats and yet they want to know how much you know. By salting your speech here and there and giving bits and pieces of your belief now and then, they will start asking you questions.

Going to the same places at the same time and day every week will expose you to others without pushing yourself the first time. Enjoy being with people. Do not immediately try to get people to come to a Bible study. Be polite and do not monopolize the conversation. If opportunity arises to interject a Bible concept, interject one into the conversation. Be yourself and make new friends. Be honest about being a Bible teacher but do not suggest giving a Bible study unless a lot of questions come up that make it a natural suggestion.

Be real and act in a manner that glorifies God. Your kind attitude and polite demeanor will make others glad to see you. These suggestions hopefully go along with your natural tendency not to be pushy. Do not have any other agenda except to love people and show you genuinely care about others. If God leads people to ask you about doing a Bible study, it will be great. If not, you are still salting conversations with God's word and that is wonderful. Be out among people and be available. Do not shy away from giving Bible studies. If you are asked, don't refuse or if enough time has passed that it is comfortable for you, bring it up.

Intentional actions to introduce Bible studies can be effective too. Every time you go to a restaurant alone, bring a Bible. Work on a Bible study so that people can see that is what you do. Be approachable. Do not be so busy that you don't see people staring at you or you don't say hi to people. Be friendly and willing to talk about what you are doing.

Alternatively, when you are out at restaurants put out a sign on your table, "Biblical questions welcome" or "need prayer please ask me". Be willing to take time with people to help them. You can even take another person with you to allow you to work on the Bible study while the other person talks to others.

Use Resources and Create Opportunities

Talk with your pastor and see if the church would be willing to give you some pew Bibles or sell you some. Churches get bulk rates, and it might be economically enough so you can give them away. Make it known that you give a free 1-hour lesson on how to use the Bible with every Bible you give out. Then give them the first Bible study lesson when you give them the Bible or if needed, arrange a time to see them after you give them the Bible. Always get their name, address, and telephone number. That way if they can't make the arranged meeting you will be able to call them and set up a new time. If you cannot make a connection at the time you give out the Bible, in the future when you start up a Bible study near them you can call them up and invite them to come to it.

Go to a bookstore and go into the spiritual section. Watch for people who look like they are searching for something and strike up a conversation. You can even go in other sections and do the same kind of thing. The idea is not to start a Bible study or even mention a Bible study immediately. But, just make friends. Find out if they're going to be back there or always come on a certain day. Then go back and just strike up another conversation.

You can devise a survey sheet about how much the average person knows about religion. Go to McDonalds or Dunkin Donuts etc. Buy coffee coupons and offer a free coupon if they take your survey. The survey does two things. First, it tells you about the makeup of the neighborhood and it gives you an opportunity to make friends. Next time you go in you can call people by their first name and go talk with them.

Have business cards made up that you can put up on poster boards. Free Bible studies – free Bibles with first lesson or advertise other clever give away products that you can put your name and telephone number on.

The First Step is Always the Hardest

Once your first study is behind you, you will already feel more at home in leading others through the Bible. The more you put yourself out there, the more at ease you will become with the amazing work you are doing in helping others. It is not always easy, people will push back on you, but I personally find strength in, and openly share, the following:

1. The Bible has been written by over 40 authors and spanning over 1600 years.
2. The Bible has been viewed critically over the centuries more times than any other book.
3. By a preponderance of evidence, it can be proven that information in the Bible should not have been known by the authors. (God breathed the Bible through the authors)
4. The Old Testament is the Jewish Bible. People who do not believe in Jesus attest to the validity of Old Testament prophecies concerning the Messiah. Isn't that just like God, the very proofs of Jesus being the Messiah are kept by irrefutable evidence because the people who attest to the validity of it do not believe in Jesus. (Over 300 prophecies).
5. There are prophecies, fore knowledge and truisms of the Bible that attest to God being the ultimate author.

Being confident in overcoming the initial denial or avoidance will lead you to those new encounters that make being a teacher all the more compelling. Having faith in the power of His word and establishing a pattern within your own method will bring you that confidence.

Final Notes

I've been asked "how long do I go on giving a Bible study to the people of each group?" The answer is that it depends on how the study started. If someone ask a question about a certain subject it may actually only be one study. Most however do not have an ending time set. They get into the habit of coming to it and enjoy the camaraderie. I do notice that if we take the summer off some people won't come back right away. Some decide not to come back at all. And that's fine. Hopefully they have stayed long enough to be studying on their own or even start their own study.

Recently, a guy from a past Bible study asked me if I'd be willing to start up again. But, I never left giving Bible studies. He of course was talking about starting up the same Bible study. That generally doesn't happen. Times change and people get into other things. My standard answer is yes I absolutely would start another study. Then I ask him to contact the other guys about when they will be free and we'll coordinate a time for it. They usually aren't able to get the same people. Some end up coming to Bible studies I have going on at the time and blend right in.

This is the beginning of a journey that transcends anything else. Teaching others to know about our Savior and God is a job that has eternal meaning. When we think of doing jobs, we normally think of things that can be accomplished in and about the lives we are living here on this earth. However, Bible study is about a far greater long lasting knowledge. Watch people change and become more of the people God wants them to be. Knowing you played a part in bringing that understanding to them is a feeling that can be had in no other way. You are on the front lines in a battle. In Sunday school, we learned a song called "Onward Christian Soldiers". It's about Christians living their daily lives for Christ. Teaching is one of the ways we can get out there are make a difference. There is nothing to compare with serving the Lord.

Chapter XV

"For I resolved to know nothing while I was with you except Jesus Christ and him crucified."
(NIV 1 Cor 2:2)

Conclusion: Insight Beyond Compare

This is the Gospel message. Sometimes we get so caught up in learning that we lose perspective on the most important thing in the Bible. Paul in Corinth limited his evangelizing to Jesus Christ and Him crucified. No correlations, no prophecy, no foreknowledge. Paul only had the Old Testament about which the gentile believers knew nothing. He had no foundation to build upon except Jesus and what had been done to Him. The most important part of Paul's message was HE'S ALIVE! He conquered death. (You find it in 1st Corinthians chapter 15).

God came to earth to live like a man and die. It was a horrible death. He died for us. Most of the people knew what happened in Paul's day. Paul had to set them straight about who Jesus was, the message He had for them (and us), and that He came back from the dead. He is alive, which means that we also will be alive after we die in this world.

In our studies, we can show people that God is real and that He has gotten us a message to let us know that fact. The Bible tells HIS STORY in a way that is totally what God want us to know to build our faith. As we learn about the Bible, our faith is built on all the things that the Bible conveys. Its complete because the Hebrews verses above lets us know that nothing else or anyone else will be sent to tell us anything new. It's all wrapped up in God's Son Jesus Christ our Lord and Savior. It is all about Him glorifying God in the Gospel story.

No one has ever spoken in simpler terms, no one has spoken in more complexity, no one has done more, been more, loved more, was more logical or cared more about mankind. All the Bible studies in the world cannot match Him or over emphasize the awe, wonderment, and power of our Savior. Never ever forget that the Bible is leading us to God and His Son. With the help of God and the Holy Spirit, God will complete His good work in us.

As we give Bible Studies, don't lose sight of our first love in all the teaching. All of our teaching should be like a drink offering to God remembering His Son's gift to us on the cross, knowing that Jesus sits at the right hand of God ever making intercessions for us. He'll come back one day to take us home with Him. So let us always think of how we can glorify God and Christ in every Bible study we give.

-Brent Mackey

There are several things that speak of the awesomeness of the Lord and the Word of God. One of these things is the insight that God shows about almost everything in creation. When touching on science, numbers, personal relationships, sin, love, greed and any number of other things God is exactly correct every time (Which should be no surprise). Let's just hit on some thought provoking Scriptures concerning attitudes and applications to daily life.

"Seldom set foot in your neighbor's house--too much of you, and he will hate you."
(NIV Prov 25:17)

"Withdraw thy foot from thy neighbour's house; lest he be weary of thee, and so hate thee."
(KJV Prov 25:17)

"What goes into a man's mouth does not make him 'unclean,' but what comes out of his mouth, that is what makes him 'unclean.'"
(NIV Matt 15:11)

"Not that which goeth into the mouth defileth a man; but that which cometh out of the mouth, this defileth a man."
(KJV Matt 15:11)

"The good man brings good things out of the good stored up in his heart, and the evil man brings evil things out of the evil stored up in his heart. For out of the overflow of his heart his mouth speaks."
(NIV Luke 6:45)

"A good man out of the good treasure of his heart bringeth forth that which is good; and an evil man out of the evil treasure of his heart bringeth forth that which is evil: for of the abundance of the heart his mouth speaketh."
(KJV Luke 6:45)

"The fear of the LORD is the beginning of
knowledge,
but fools despise wisdom and discipline."
(NIV Prov 1:7)

The fear of the LORD is the beginning of
knowledge: but fools despise wisdom and
instruction.
(KJV Prov 1:7)

"The rich rule over the poor, and the borrower is
servant to the lender."
(NIV Prov 22:7)

"The rich ruleth over the poor, and the borrower is
servant to the lender."
(KJV Prov 22:7)

"A hot-tempered man stirs up dissension, but a
patient man calms a quarrel."
(NIV Prov 15:18)

"A wrathful man stirreth up strife: but he that is slow
to anger appeaseth strife."
(KJV Prov 15:18)

The Bible is such a wealth of information. On every page you will find prophecies, fore knowledge, insightful truisms, and wisdom only God could have lavished so plentifully for us to feast on and learn from. And of course, most importantly we find His Son. With study, we find that in a very real way the Bible is about Him and His sacrifice for us. What a wonderful merciful God we have!

Throughout your quest to give quality Bible studies, remember that people come from different backgrounds and experience. You may find some startling revelations about people and the way that they think and learn. You may also find that people have different ideas and opinions. Embrace these differences and the newness that you find in the students that attend the Bible study. Be flexible an open concerning different maturity levels and needs that the students may require.

Remember that God is the great teacher. His word will inspire and lift the spirits of men beyond belief. As you study with your group remember

God's word is sufficient, he will build the people's faith through hearing just as the Bible says. Just do the very best that you can in preparation and love. Your class will surprise you and enliven you as well.

Always be a Berean and check out the answers – make up some questions of your own and have a great time learning and giving Bible studies.

> **"As soon as it was night, the brothers sent Paul and Silas away to Berea. On arriving there, they went to the Jewish synagogue. [11] Now the Bereans were of more noble character than the Thessalonians, for they received the message with great eagerness and examined the Scriptures every day to see if what Paul said was true."**
> **(NIV Acts 17:10, 11)**

> **"And the brethren immediately sent away Paul and Silas by night unto Berea: who coming thither went into the synagogue of the Jews. [11] These were more noble than those in Thessalonica, in that they received the word with all readiness of mind, and searched the scriptures daily, whether those things were so."**
> **(KJV Acts 17:10, 11)**

Please notice that Bereans searched daily to find out if what Paul said was true. They didn't search to see whether his word was false. This means that they searched with a positive attitude to make certain what they thought was true was indeed true. Some take the opposite view and try to prove that what is being said is false. The negative approach will always find some small thing to find fault with and miss the overwhelming amount of facts that substantiate the truth. It's because their goal is not to find the truth. The goal is to substantiate the fact that they believed it was a lie. It is amazing the length that people will go to prove themselves correct when their premise is based on negativity.

When teaching, always approach ideas and comments with the air of possibility. If you find that concepts are wrong, you will have exhausted all possibilities that they are right. It has a much different appearance in front of other people. It will always change to a more humble approach.

Enjoy teaching, enjoy people learning and understand that you are giving out the message and the Holy Spirit will give the increase. Your responsibility is in giving out the Word of God the best way that you can.

Be happy and joyful as you are doing one of the most important jobs that you can do, Glorifying God!

Bible Studies

The following pages will include "ready to give" Bible studies. Except for the first study, each Bible study will include a student's page of questions as well as a teacher's page with the answers and notes. These are meant to be "stand alone" Bible studies, one that you could use in evangelizing or starting up a Bible study. Some have a notation to a corresponding chapter used to illustrate a principle talked about in that chapter.

The best way to use these Bible studies is to take them yourself first. Note each answer you gave in correspondence with the teacher notes. Write down anything that excites your mind and remember that you didn't know that before you took the lesson. Then every time before you give the study look back at your notes and remember the feeling of awestruck wonder you had when you learned some points you may not have known. Realize that you will be giving a study to other people, who will have similar feelings to what you had when you took it.

Bible Study #1

The Beginners First Study

The first Bible study is about either evangelizing or is used as the first Bible study I give any new group starting up. It is the first because it answers the question "Did God really inspire the Bible to be written?" and "How do we know?" If I use it to evangelize, I will only use a portion of the study that I feel is most appropriate for the person to whom I'm speaking. These instances usually come about by bringing up the Bible in some interesting, unthreatening way. If it is used as a scheduled Bible study, then I will use it exactly as it's written, point-by-point.

Evangelizing can take place in many different settings. Restaurants, homes and even at the work place providing it is allowed on lunch breaks. Some of my beginning conversations include the question "If I can show you that God inspired the Bible to be written and He has something He wants you to know, would you want to see it?" Another opening is to say, "I was reading something that knocked me off my feet. Can I show it to you?" Then I would usually ask them if they had a Bible I could borrow (If I'm in their home). By borrowing their Bible, they will have confidence that you are being sincere and it's not some kind of a cult thing. Or if you're out just get one from your car. Some of these meetings are scheduled to talk about the Bible but when they are only conversational meetings and the topic comes up you don't want to already be prepared with you Bible as if your meeting was exclusively for the purpose of witnessing to them.

This system has helped me talk to literally hundreds of people about the Lord. By using one or two things in the "First Study," I piqued the interest of an enormous amount of people. Of course, it should always be remembered that God is the one who draws the people. He is also the one who will give us opportunities to talk with people. Therefore, the reality is that it is God alone who makes things happen. However, if we take the time to learn things and make ourselves available it is God's decision concerning the opportunities we have to witness to people. It's our responsibility to open our mouths and talk to people wherever the opportunity arises.

This lesson is concerning a conversation about the Bible and showing people why they should believe that God inspired the Bible to be written. Why we believe what we believe is the first step toward people being sincerely involved with Bible studies as opposed to hoping we will leave their house soon.

So, the one thing that sums up the way to present this study and how it should be given is the word "explanation". We are explaining about the Bible NOT trying to get them to come to our church or "be saved". We are explaining some great facts about why the Bible has been inspired by God. The same way that you would kind of brag about you father or mother. You are showing them why it can be seen that God inspired the Bible to be written. That's all. You are telling the truth. If it results in giving them more studies or coming to your church or just wets the appetite for someone else to build it's all good. Please don't do it with any other idea or goal in mind. Just explain to them what you know.

The entire Bible study is given as if you were going to be spending 45 minutes or so in someone's house over coffee. Use the information or just parts of the information appropriate to the situation you are in at the time of an initial conversation.

Outline to 1st Lesson – Apologetics

I. Warm up – Introduction of ideas
   A. Potential questions (I don't usually ask all of them)
      1. What have you heard about the Bible?
      2. Do you feel the Bible was really inspired by God?
      3. What does it mean that everything in the Bible was actually inspired by God?
      4. Is the Bible different from any other "Holy Book"?
      5. Do you feel Christianity is the only way to get to God?
      6. Do you feel the Bible has changed over the years?
   B. Logic statements leading to apologetics
      1. We need to be confident that the Bible is really God's word.
      2. There is an absolute truth that we can depend on and have faith in.
      3. We need to go beyond theory and actually prove to ourselves that there really is a God and He has provided a way for us to know it.
II. The Bible (Points to show the Bible is reliable)
   A. Read and explain Old testament piece (Following outline)
      1. Start at the top
      2. End at – "which we need have any doubt" – ½ way down page
      3. Read and explain New Testament piece (Following outline)
      4. Do not read all the comparisons (I use Plato and Aristotle only)
      5. Explain comparison and ask how many early manuscripts of the New Testament they feel are around today
      6. Finish read at "300 to 400 years".
   B. Bible history
      1. Written over a 1600-year period at least
      2. Written by over 40 authors
      3. Give out piece on time and authors of the Bible (Not included)
      4. Give brief explanation of the Bible (Table of contents)
   C. Bible proofs – how God lets us know the Bible's inspired
      1. The Bible explains things unknown to the author
      2. Isaiah 40:22 God sits on the circle of the earth (approx. 700 BC)
      3. Job 26:7 God hangs the earth on nothing (pre-dates Moses 1450 BC)
      4. Correlate Columbus 2200 years later and the world being flat– Atlas holding up the world and ancient maps saying turtles held up the earth.
      5. No myths in the Bible –why?
      6. Genesis 22:17 stars as numerous as the sands on the seashore – cannot be counted.
      7. Correlate with Galileo 1st time unable to count the stars 3600 plus years later when the telescope was first invented
      8. Mention all the laws concerning health and hygiene and the fact that the black plague was halted in Europe by following the Biblical quarantine laws.

D. Prophecies in the Bible – read Isaiah 46:8-10 (No other book can compare to the Bible no other faith can stand under the stated criteria for belief) Examples of just a few prophecies:
1. Micah 5:2
2. Psalm 22:1 and 14-18
3. Zechariah 11: 12, 13 – save the place, go to Matthew 27:3-7, go back, and read Zech. Passage

Note[8]: I find the most effective way to present the prophecies is by reading them and asking the people who the passage is talking about. Then explain when it was written and by who – or have them look up the date in a handout (About dates and authors of the Bible) for themselves if it's available (II - A. and B.). For D. I explain how compounded prophecies are so much harder to predict, and I ask who could have known the simple prophecies let alone the more complex ones hundreds of years before. I finish by explaining there are over 300 such prophecies in the Old Testament about Christ.

I usually end with statement about how excited I am whenever I read the Bible because I can really see that only God could have inspired such foreknowledge and simple yet complex ideas throughout the entire text. It is something outside of our realm of comprehension.

Challenge: Take any part of the Bible and say the verse better, clearer using less words to convey the exact same thought. You can't! With the variety of writers, how is that possible?

How come there are only truths in the Bible and no myths. Thunder and lightning are not mentioned as the god's being angry at each other etc.

The two pieces I read to people are on the following pages (Just read smaller sections so they get the meat of the articles)

Validity of the Old Testament

Robert D. Wilson was a Princeton Professor, a noted scholar and was fluent in over 40 Semitic languages. As one of the best language scholars ever to exist, he concluded after extensive review and research in his book, "Scientific Investigation of the Old Testament," the Following:

> For 45 years continuously…I have devoted myself to the one great study of the Old Testament, in all its languages, in all its archaeology, in all its translations…
> The critics of the Bible who go to it in order to find fault…claim to themselves all knowledge and all virtue and all love of truth. One of their

---

[8] These are my notes. Research your own prophecies or science facts, or just use mine. Be sure to use your own words and understanding to explain it to people.

favorite phrases is, "All scholars agree." When a man says that…I wish to know who the scholars are and why they agree. Where do they get their evidence…? I defy any man to make an attack upon the Old Testament on the ground of evidence that I cannot investigate…

After I learned the necessary languages I set about the investigation of every consonant in the Hebrew Old Testament. There are about a million and a quarter of these; and it took me many years to achieve my task. I had to observe the variations of the text…in the manuscripts, or in the notes of the Massoretes…or in the various versions or in the parallel passages or in the conjectural emendations of critics; and then I had to classify the results…to reduce the Old Testament criticism to an absolutely objective science; something which is based on evidence, and not opinion…

The result of those 45 yrs' study which I have given to the text has been this: I can affirm that there is not a page of the Old Testament concerning which we need have any doubt… (for example to illustrate it's accuracy): There are 29 ancient kings whose names are mentioned not only in the Bible but also on monument of their own time…There are 195 consonants in these 29 proper names. Yet we find that in the documents of the Hebrew Old Testament there are only 2 or 3 out of the entire 195 about which there can be any question of their being written in exactly the same way as they were inscribed on their own monuments (which archaeologists have to date discovered). Some of these go back 4,000 years and are so written that every letter is clear and correct…

Compare this accuracy with…the greatest scholar of his age, the librarian at Alexandria in 200 B.C.. He compiled a catalogue of the kings of Egypt, 38 in all. Of the entire number only 3 or 4 are recognizable. He also made a list of the king of Assyria; in only 1 case can we tell who is meant; and that one is not spelt correctly. Or take Ptolemy, who drew up a register of 18 kings of Babylon. Not one of them is properly spelt; you could not make them out at all if you did not know from other sources to what he is referring.

If anyone talks about the Bible, ask him about the kings mentioned in it. There are 29 kings referred to, and 10 different countries among these 29; all of which are included in the Bible and on monuments. Every one of these is given his right name in the Bible, his right country, and placed in correct chronological order. Think what that means

While the study of the religious systems of the ancient peoples has shown that there was amongst them a groping after God, nowhere is it to be seen that they reached any clear apprehension of the One True God, the Creator, Preserver, Judge, Savior an Sanctifier of His people. Their religions were of an outward kind; the Old Testament religion is essentially one of the mind and heart; a religion of love, joy, faith, hope, and salvation through the grade of God. How can we account for this?

The prophets of Israel declared that their teachings came from God. The modern critical school is antagonistic to this claim. They say that the prophets gave utterance to the ideas of their own time, and that they were

limited by their environment. But, if this is so how does it come about that neither from the oracles of Thebes and Memphis, nor from Delphi and Rome, nor from Babylon, nor from the deserts of Media, but from the sheep-folds and humble homes of Israel, yea, from the captive by the river of an alien land, came forth those great messages of hope and salvation?
(Robert D. Wilson 1856-1930)

Is the Bible Reliable?

Biblical scholar F.F. Bruce writes "There is no body of ancient literature in the world which enjoys such a wealth of good textual attestation as the New Testament." J. Harold Greenlee (1964 An Introduction to New Testament Textual Criticism) explains:

"The number of available manuscripts of the New Testament is overwhelmingly greater than those of any work of ancient literature...and the earliest extant manuscripts of the New testament were written much closer to the date of the original writing..." For the sake of comparison, here are some well accepted, ancient secular works showing the author, the date written, the number of manuscripts surviving, and the earliest manuscript:

Sophocles	496-406 B.C.	100	1400 yrs
Herodotus	480-425 B.C.	8	1300 yrs
Euripides	480-406 B.C.	9	1500 yrs
Thucydides	460-400 B.C.	8	1300 yrs
Plato	427-327 B.C.	7	1200 yrs
Aristotle	384-322 B.C.	5	1400 yrs
Demosthenes	383-322 B.C.	200	1300 yrs
Caesar	100-44 B.C.	10	1000 yrs
Lucretius	60 B.C.	2	1600 yrs
Tacitus	100 A.D.	20	1000 yrs

In contrast, there are about 24,600 copies of the New Testament manuscripts, some of which date back within a century of the originals and many others within about 300 to 400 years. Then why does one continually hear the false claim that the biblical manuscripts are not reliable? The fact that this lie persists in academic circles demonstrates the extreme prejudice against the Bible because of what it says. God's Word convicts the conscience. How interesting that questions about the accuracy of the manuscripts are never raised for other ancient writings- unless they offer proof of the Bible's validity. "The Antiquities of the Jews," by Josephus, offers considerable verification of the New Testament and the life and death of Jesus, so it too comes under vicious attack.

The Bible is the most quoted book in the world, in thousands of times more so than any secular work. That is not only true today but has always been the case. Consequently, one can reproduce the entire New Testament and much of the Old Testament by quotations contained in personal letters and epistles written within a century after Christ commissioned His disciples to preach the Gospel.

(Dave Hunt, "In Defense of The Faith" Pg. 71
Published July 1st 1996 by Harvest House Publishers.)

The foundation for Bible being the inspiration of God has been explained, in hopefully a fun and exciting way. This should be given in a manner of excitement showing the things that are really interesting.

Bible study #2

Snake in the desert

The snake in the desert is an excellent Bible study to illustrate typology in the Bible. Typology is when a person, thing or event (Or combination of these items) in the Old Testament is being identified by the New Testament as being like something that is in the new Testament (See chapter IX, page 105). When this happens, the object, person or event is said to be a type. Phrases containing words like "prefigures," "type," "just as," as, or "like" alert you to these occurrences.

Let me give you an illustration:

> **"Just as Moses lifted up the snake in the desert, so**
> **the Son of Man must be lifted up, that everyone who**
> **believes in him may have eternal life."**
> **(NIV John 3:14-15)**

> **"And as Moses lifted up the serpent in the**
> **wilderness, even so must the Son of man be lifted up:**
> **That whosoever believeth in him should not perish,**
> **but have eternal life."**
> **(KJV John 3:14, 15)**

In John above, we see that the Bible identifies an event recorded in the Bible by Moses during the wilderness march as being similar to Jesus being lifted up.

Briefly, the idea is that in the wilderness march God sent a plague of snakes to bite and kill the Israelites because they rebelled which led them into sin. Moses went before God and made a plea for the Israelites. God heard Moses prayer, and had Moses make a brazen serpent he was to put on a pole to be lifted up so the people could see it. When the snakes bit people, God told Moses to have them go and look up at the snake. When they did, they were healed of the poison that would have killed them.

Jesus said in John, the Son of man was going to be lifted up like this serpent. Therefore, the serpent becomes a "Type" of Christ. Because the New Testament said it was. Below is the Bible study on this subject.

Outline to Lesson- The Brazen Serpent

Can you guess the ten plagues that God brought on Egypt?

Do you think that the Israelites realized the power and reality of God?

Would you have believed that God was a reality if you were there?

With all this verification, why would people turn away from God?

> **"They traveled from Mount Hor along the route to the Red Sea, to go around Edom. But, the people grew impatient on the way; they spoke against God and against Moses, and said, "Why have you brought us up out of Egypt to die in the desert? There is no bread! There is no water! And we detest this miserable food!"**
> **Then the LORD sent venomous snakes among them; they bit the people and many Israelites died. The people came to Moses and said, "We sinned when we spoke against the LORD and against you. Pray that the LORD will take the snakes away from us." So Moses prayed for the people.**
> **The LORD said to Moses, "Make a snake and put it up on a pole; anyone who is bitten can look at it and live."[9] So Moses made a bronze snake and put it up on a pole. Then when anyone was bitten by a snake and looked at the bronze snake, he lived."**
> **(NIV Numbers 21:4-9)**

So why do you think the above incident occurred?

Do you think that the people forgot about God?

Numbers 21:4-9 - The Bronze Snake

1. Where did the people of Israel become impatient? (21:4)

2. How did the people express their impatience against God and Moses? (21:5)

3. What kind of punishment did the Lord give the Israelites for being impatient? (21:6)

4. How did the people ask Moses to intervene on their behalf? (21:7)

5. What did the Lord tell Moses to do with a snake? (21:8)

6. If a snake bit someone, how could he or she be healed? (21:9)

7. What do you think the people thought about when this incident took place?

"He removed the high places, smashed the sacred stones and cut down the Asherah poles. He broke into pieces the bronze snake Moses had made, for up to that time the Israelites had been burning incense to it. (It was called Nehushtan.)"
(NIV 2 Kings 18:4)

8. Why do you think that God chose to include Hezekiah taking down the bronze snake in the Bible?

Here is another verse about the snake:

(Jesus said this to Nicodemus)
"Just as Moses lifted up the snake in the desert, so the Son of Man must be lifted up, that everyone who believes in him may have eternal life."
(NIV John 3:14-15)

The things the snake in the desert have in common with the Lord and what He's done for us:

9. What does the serpent represent in the Old Testament?

10. If the serpent represents that what would be represented by its bite?

11. If the serpents bite cause death, what would that bite cause?

12. What does it mean to look up at the serpent and be healed in context of Jesus being lifted up?

13. Did the people have to do anything to be healed in the wilderness?

14. Do believers have to do anything to be cleansed and redeemed?

15. Why do you think that Christ used this idea to align himself?

Often we find exactly the idea of Jesus, His life, and or circumstances in the pages of the Old Testament. Do you think it was mere coincidence?

Teacher's notes: The Brazen Serpent

Can you guess the ten plagues that God brought on Egypt?

The first plague—water turned to blood

The second plague—frogs

The third plague—lice

The fourth plague—flies

The fifth plague—murrain (dead cattle by plague not the Israelites cattle though)

The sixth plague—boils

The seventh plague—hail

The eight plagues—locusts

The ninth plague—darkness

The tenth plague—death of the firstborn

Do you think that the Israelites realized the power and reality of God? (*Yes*)

Would you have believed that God was a reality if you were there? (*Yes*)

Note: There are several examples early on the wilderness march with Moses where people saw miracles up front and personal. Of course, the parting of the Red Sea was a big miracle but here is a couple of others that were just as telling.

> **"By day the LORD went ahead of them in a pillar of cloud to guide them on their way and by night in a pillar of fire to give them light, so that they could travel by day or night. Neither the pillar of cloud by day nor the pillar of fire by night left its place in front of the people."**
> **(Exodus 13:21-22)**

> **"During the forty years that I led you through the desert, your clothes did not wear out, nor did the sandals on your feet.**
> **So not only did they see miracles but they kept on seeing them every day. Not to mention the manna from Heaven every morning etc."**
> **(Deut. 29:5)**

So why do you think the following incident occurred?

> **"They traveled from Mount Hor along the route to
> the Red Sea, to go around Edom. But, the people
> grew impatient on the way; they spoke against God
> and against Moses, and said, "Why have you
> brought us up out of Egypt to die in the desert?
> There is no bread! There is no water! And we detest
> this miserable food!"
> Then the LORD sent venomous snakes among
> them; they bit the people and many Israelites died.
> The people came to Moses and said, "We sinned
> when we spoke against the LORD and against you.
> Pray that the LORD will take the snakes away from
> us. "So Moses prayed for the people.
> The LORD said to Moses, "Make a snake and put it
> up on a pole; anyone who is bitten can look at it and
> live." So Moses made a bronze snake and put it up
> on a pole. Then when anyone was bitten by a snake
> and looked at the bronze snake, he lived."
> (NIV Numbers 21:4-9)**

Do you think that the people forgot about God? (*No – they took Him for
granted and minimized His importance*)

Numbers 21:4-9 - The Bronze Snake

1. Where did the people of Israel become impatient?
    (21:4) (*They were going around the Land of Edom starting at
    Mt. Hor by the way of the Red Sea.*)

2. How did the people express their impatience against
    God and Moses? (21:5) (*Spoke against Him and Moses*)

3. What kind of punishment did the Lord give the
    Israelites for being impatient? (21:6) (*God sent fiery
    snakes among the people and killed the people by biting them*)

4. How did the people ask Moses to intervene on their
    behalf? (21:7) (*Admitted guilt and ask Moses to intercede
    for them*)

5. What did the Lord tell Moses to do with a bronze snake? (21:8) (*Put it on the pole*)

6. If a snake bit someone, how could he or she be healed? (21:9) (*Go look at the brazen snake.*)

7. What do you think the people thought about when this incident took place? (*First they did something wrong and sinned against God. Because of what God did, the people may have realized that God had total supremacy over the snakes and everything else even life and death.*)

Another story about the snake was

> **"He removed the high places, smashed the sacred stones, and cut down the Asherah poles. He broke into pieces the bronze snake Moses had made, for up to that time the Israelites had been burning incense to it." (It was called Nehushtan.)**
> **(NIV 2 Kings 18:4)**

8. Why do you think that God chose to include Hezekiah taking down the bronze snake? (*He doesn't want us to make a mistake and think that sin (worshipping a snake) goes unpunished there is another reason and that is to show the human nature of man. Man has a tendency to worship almost anything, which is wrong. This idea of the brazen snake being worshiped is probably one of the reasons that the Lord didn't allow the original manuscripts to survive – we'd probably be worshipping them too. God doesn't want us to worship anything other than God Himself.*)

Here is another verse about the snake:

> **"Just as Moses lifted up the snake in the desert, so the Son of Man must be lifted up, [15] that everyone who believes in him may have eternal life."**
> **(NIV John 3:14, 15)**

The things the snake in the desert has in common with the Lord and what He's done for us:

9. What does the serpent represent in the Old Testament? (*Satan and evil*)

10. If the serpent represents that what would be represented by its bite? (*Sin*)

11. If the serpents bite caused death what would an evil bite cause? (*Spiritual death*)

12. What does it mean to look up at the serpent and be healed in context of Jesus being lifted up? (*If we look to Jesus we will be saved from the bite of sin*)

13. Did the people have to do anything else to be healed in the wilderness? (*No*)

14. Do believers have to do anything else to be cleansed and redeemed? (*No*)

15. Why do you think that Christ used this idea to align himself? (*The idea of being represented by the symbol of Satan or evil becomes more appropriate if you realize that Jesus took on all the sins of the world – He actually became sin for us – thus in a sense the portrayal of evil*)

"God made him who had no sin to be sin for us, so that in him we might become the righteousness of God."
(NIV 2 Cor. 5:21)

"For what the law was powerless to do in that it was weakened by the sinful nature, God did by sending his own Son in the likeness of sinful man to be a sin offering. And so he condemned sin in sinful man,"
(NIV Romans 8:3)

Often we find exactly the idea of Jesus, His life, and or circumstances in the pages of the Old Testament. Do you think it was mere coincidence?

There are several examples of "Typology" in the New Testament. The lesson about water from the rock certainly does have the same things and is identified as a type in 1st Corinthians.

Bible Study #3:

Getting water out of a rock

Let me illustrate the idea of teaching and correlating the inspiration of God with a Scripture about obeying God. This is also another study of typology.

We're going to look at the time period when Moses was leading the children of Israel during the wilderness march.

First of all, read Exodus 17:1-7 and also Numbers 20:1-13

After reading the above passages take the following Bible study.

Student's Questions –

Read Exodus 17:1-17:7 - In the Desert

1. What did the people complain to Moses about? (17:1-2)

2. Why did Moses say, "Why do you test the Lord"?

3. How serious was the complaint?

4. What was the threat?

5. Who did Moses cry out to?

6. What was Moses afraid of?

7. What did the Lord tell Moses to do?

8. What did God tell Moses He would do?

9. Did Moses do exactly what he was told to do?

10. Did this take courage and faith on the part of Moses to do it?

11. Did the Lord prove that He was with them as verse 7 asks?

12. So, do you think that we should test God?

Now let's look at Numbers 20:1-13

13. What did the people complain to Moses about? (17:1-2)

14. Did Moses say, "Why do you test the Lord"?

15. How serious was the complaint?

16. If something weren't done what would happen?

17. What did Moses do to get God's attention?

18. Did Moses have to say anything before God spoke?

19. What did the Lord say Moses was to do?

20. What did God say He would do?
21. Did Moses do what he was told to do?

22. What did Moses do?

23. Was Moses given a punishment? What?

24. Do you feel this was a harsh punishment?

25. Is Exodus and Numbers about the same event?

26. Can you list some differences between the two passages?

Notice some similarities to some things in the New Testament in these two accounts

27. How many times was Christ struck?

28. How many times did God want the rock struck?

29. Once our Lord was smitten for us and we come to Him and make Him our Lord and Savior, what are we supposed to do if we sin?

30. What was Moses to do the second time concerning the rock?

31. Where was God when Moses struck the rock the first time?

32. Where was God during the crucifixion?

33. Is there any similarity between the people that were present at the rock and the crucifixion?

34. What did God mean when He said that- "Moses didn't treat Him as Holy in front of sons of Israel" after Moses struck the rock twice?

35. Do you think God punished Moses more harshly because he not only disobeyed but he also broke the "type" at the second rock by striking it twice?

Teacher /leader's copy

Getting water out of a rock

We're going to look at the time period when Moses was leading the children of Israel during the wilderness march.

First of all, read Exodus 17:1-7 and then Numbers 20:1-13

Exodus 17:1-17:7 - In the Desert

1. What did the people complain to Moses about? (17:1-2) (*The people had run out of water*)

2. Why did Moses say, "Why do you test the Lord"? (*The people were losing faith with God – they should have known He would provide for their needs without trying to test God their own way*)

3. How serious was the complaint? (*Very serious – water was necessary to their very life*)

4. What was the threat? (*They would certainly die*)

5. Who did Moses cry out to? (*He cried out to God*)

6. What was Moses afraid of? (*That the people would kill him*)

7. What did the Lord say Moses was to do?

**"The LORD answered Moses, "Walk on ahead of the people. Take with you some of the elders of Israel and take in your hand the staff with which you struck the Nile, and go.
…Strike the rock, and water will come out of it for the people to drink."
(NIV Exodus 17:5, 6)**

"And the LORD said unto Moses, go on before the people, and take with thee of the elders of Israel; and

thy rod, wherewith thou smotest the river, take in thine hand, and go.
Behold, I will stand before thee there upon the rock in Horeb; and thou shalt smite the rock, and there shall come water out of it that the people may drink. And

Moses did so in the sight of the elders of Israel."
(KJV Exodus 17:5, 6)

8. What did God say He would do?

Exodus 17:6
"I will stand there before you by the rock at Horeb."
(NIV Exodus 17:6)

"Behold, I will stand before thee there upon the rock in Horeb;"
(KJV Exodus 17:6)

9. Did Moses do exactly what he was told to do? (*Yes*)

10. Did it take courage and faith on the part of Moses to do it? (*Yes – he risked loss of leadership, embarrassment, and prophet status and probably his life.*)

11. Did the Lord prove that He was with them as verse 7 asks? (*Absolutely*)

12. So, do you think that we should test God?

"Luke 4:12 Jesus answered the last temptation by Satan by saying "You shall not put the Lord your God to the test."
(NIV Luke 4:12)

"And Jesus answering said unto him, it is said, thou shalt not tempt the Lord thy God."
(KJV Luke 4:12)

Now let's look at Numbers 20:1-13

13. What did the people complain to Moses about? (17:1-2) (*The people had run out of water*)

14. Did Moses say, "Why do you test the Lord"? (*No*)

15. How serious was the complaint? (*Very serious – water was necessary to their very life*)

16. If something weren't done what would happen? (*They would certainly die*)

17. What did Moses do to get God's attention? (*Aaron and Moses went to the doorway of the tent of meeting and fell on their faces*)

18. Did Moses have to say anything before God spoke? (*No*)

19. What did the Lord say Moses was to do?

"Take the staff, and you and your brother Aaron gather the assembly together. Speak to that rock before their eyes and it will pour out its water. You will bring water out of the rock for the community so they and their livestock can drink."
(NIV Numbers 20:8)

"Take the rod, and gather thou the assembly together, thou, and Aaron thy brother, and speak ye unto the rock before their eyes; and it shall give forth his water, and thou shalt bring forth to them water out of the rock: so thou shalt give the congregation and their beasts drink."
(KJV Numbers 20:8)

20. What did God say He would do? (*He doesn't say*)

21. Did Moses do what he was told to do? (*No*)

22. What did Moses do? (*Yelled at the people and struck the rock twice*)

23. Was Moses given a punishment? What? (*Yes. – He couldn't go into the promised land*)

"But the LORD said to Moses and Aaron, "Because you did not trust in me enough to honor me as holy in the sight of the Israelites, you will not bring this community into the land I give them."
(NIV Numbers 20:12)

"And the LORD spake unto Moses and Aaron, because ye believed me not, to sanctify me in the eyes of the children of Israel, therefore ye shall not bring this congregation into the land which I have given them."
(KJV Numbers 20:12)

At this point, it's important to talk about obeying God and his commandments. You need to make students realize that obeying God has it benefits as well as consequences if we do not obey them. So when talking about punishments, bring up points about fairness and how Moses was obedient. Point out what could have caused him to disobey God. After that, let's start to look at the awesomeness of God.

24. Do you feel this was a harsh punishment? (*Yes, – but fitting for not doing what God explicitly Told Moses to do.*)

25. Is Exodus and Numbers about the same event? (*No*)

26. Can you list some differences between the two passages?

    1. *God said strike the rock versus speak to the rock*

    2. *God said pass before the people and take some of the elders with you Versus assemble the congregation*

    3. *God said he would stand before him on the rock at Horeb versus not saying anything*

    4. *Moses followed instructions and struck the rock versus Moses disobeyed and struck the rock twice*

5. *Moses wasn't punished versus extreme punishment*

As previously mentioned the New Testament sheds light on the Old Testament. It is said that the Old Testament is the New Testament concealed and the New Testament is the Old Testament revealed.

Going along with these ideas and knowing that we need to get our light from the New Testament, we learn things that can help us understand why these two accounts are in the Old Testament if we look into the New Testament. Let's look at 1st Corinthians

> **"For I do not want you to be ignorant of the fact, brothers, that our forefathers were all under the cloud and that they all passed through the sea. They were all baptized into Moses in the cloud and in the sea. They all ate the same spiritual food and drank the same spiritual drink; for they drank from the spiritual rock that accompanied them, and that rock was Christ."**
> **(NIV 1 Cor. 10:1-4)**

> **"Moreover, brethren, I would not that ye should be ignorant, how that all our fathers were under the cloud, and all passed through the sea; And were all baptized unto Moses in the cloud and in the sea; And did all eat the same spiritual meat; And did all drink the same spiritual drink: for they drank of that spiritual Rock that followed them: and that Rock was Christ."**
> **(KJV 1 Cor. 10:1-4)**

Knowing that the rock they drank from was a picture of Christ let's look at some things God may have wanted done to treat the rock in a similar way to Christ.

Notice some similarities to some things in the New Testament in these two accounts

27. How many times was Christ struck? (*Once for all*)

28. How many times did God want the rock struck? (*Once*)

"Prophecy about Christ

> Surely he took up our infirmities
> and carried our sorrows,
> yet we considered him stricken by God,
> smitten by him, and afflicted."
> (NIV Isaiah 53:4)

Speaking of Christ as our High Priest and His sacrifice in Hebrews:

> "But when this priest had offered for all time one
> sacrifice for sins, he sat down at the right hand of
> God."
> (NIV Hebrews 10:12)

> "But this man, after he had offered one sacrifice for
> sins forever, sat down on the righthand of God;"
> (KJV Hebrews 10:12)

29. Once our Lord was smitten for us and we come to Him and make Him our Lord and Savior, what are we supposed to do if we sin? (*Speak to Christ in confession*)

> "If we confess our sins, he is faithful and just and
> will forgive us our sins and purify us from all
> unrighteousness."
> (NIV 1 John 1:9)

> "If we confess our sins, he is faithful and just to
> forgive us our sins, and to cleanse us from all
> unrighteousness."
> (KJV 1 John 1:9)

30. What was Moses to do the second time concerning the rock? (*He was supposed to speak to the rock*)

31. Where was God when Moses struck the rock the first time? (*Standing right by the rock*)

32. Where was God during the crucifixion? (*He wasn't with Christ in an intimate way but He was there because God is everywhere – so He was right there watching and knowing--*

He was allowing His son to be smitten that we might be cleansed of sins and have eternal life)

"Where can I go from your Spirit?
Where can I flee from your presence?
If I go up to the Heavens, you are there;
if I make my bed in the depths, you are there.
If I rise on the wings of the dawn,
if I settle on the far side of the sea,
even there your hand will guide me,
your right hand will hold me fast."
(NIV Psalm 139:7-10)

The old testament prophetic Psalm about the crucifixion started with

"My God My God why have you forsaken me?"
(Psalm 22:1)

Jesus said on the cross

"My God, My God why have you forsaken me?"
(NIV Mark 15:34)

"And at the ninth hour Jesus cried with a loud voice, saying, Eloi, Eloi, lama sabachthani? which is, being interpreted, My God, my God, why hast thou forsaken me?"
(KJV Mark 15:34)

33. Is there any similarity between the people that were present at the rock and the crucifixion? (*Very similar at the first rock it was elders and people, at the second rock it was just people. The elders were present at the crucifixion when Christ saved us by his life giving sacrifice of being struck, but the elders need not be present during the prayers of the saints when we ask Christ to forgive our sins - we speak to Christ personally with our confessions.*)

34. What did God mean when He said that- "Moses didn't treat Him as Holy in front of sons of Israel" after Moses struck the rock twice? (*It must have been prophetic of Christ because Christ was supposed to be struck only once, the rock should not have been struck twice as it*

wasn't necessary – so Moses should have treated him (the Rock) with reverence and as holy because Christ is holy because He is God. Or God spoke directly to Moses and Moses treated God without reverence or Holy because he disobeyed Him)

35. Do you think God punished Moses more harshly because he not only disobeyed but he also broke the "type" at the second rock by striking it twice? (*I think so*)

The most important similarity is that the rock in both instances gave the children of Israel life by having life giving water flow from it the first time water flowed from the rock after it was struck and the second time it would have had living water flow from it by just speaking to it. By living water, I mean that without that water flowing from the rock they Israelites would have died.

Without Christ's death on the cross and without us being able to come to Him for forgiveness we also would be dead. The first example (Old Testament) was a physical death – but the second is far more important Christ saves us from a spiritual death forever. Christ really is our rock of salvation. The living water is the Word of God and as God incarnate the Living Word is Christ Himself for He is the Word of God in the flesh.

Notice John 4:10-14

"Jesus answered her, "If you knew the gift of God and who it is that asks you for a drink, you would have asked him and he would have given you living water."
"Sir," the woman said, "you have nothing to draw with and the well is deep. Where can you get this living water? Are you greater than our father Jacob, who gave us the well and drank from it himself, as did also his sons and his flocks and herds?"
Jesus answered, "Everyone who drinks this water will be thirsty again, but whoever drinks the water I give him will never thirst. Indeed, the water I give him will become in him a spring of water welling up to eternal life."
(NIV John 4:10-14)

Do you see how the awesomeness of God in foreknowledge, teaching and prophecy? The Bible comes alive when people start to realize that God really did inspire it to be written. The very words of the Bible start to mean greater things. The ideas and promises start to be depended upon because people see the awesomeness of God's inspiration contained in the Bible.

Bible study #4

A Study on Abraham and Isaac

This Bible study is a great example of a similarity in the Old Testament and the New Testament. Although not specifically called out as typology you will find that the events that take place are similar to the events of the New Testament.

I've broken this up into two different parts. Due to the amount of information, it will take up two Bible studies if not more to get through it.

List of Scriptures to read/use:

Part 1 Scriptures
   Genesis 12:6-7
   Genesis 15:1-6
   Genesis 17:15-17
   Genesis 18:1…14
   Genesis 21:1-5
   Genesis 22:1-19

Part 2 Scriptures
   Genesis 24:1-11
   Genesis 24:34-36
   Genesis 24:62-67

Outline to Lesson- A Study on Abraham and Isaac

Part 1 questions

Genesis 12: 7

    1.   What does God promise Abraham?

    2.   Does this mean that Abraham will have at least one child from Sarah?

Genesis 15: 1-6

    3.   Has a significant time passed between the above promise and this verse? (1-3)

    4.   Who is the one Abram says will inherit his property? (2)

    5.   Does God repeat a similar promise as in chapter 12 above? (4,5)

    6.   What was credited to Abram as righteousness? (6)

    7.   How important was Abram's faith? How important is our faith today?

Genesis 17:15-22

    8.   Why do you think that God changed Sarah's name? (15)

    9.   Why did Abraham laugh to himself when God told him about a son? (17)

    10. What was the child's name to be and when would Sarah have him? (19, 21)

Genesis 18:1-14

    11. Did the Lord appear to Abraham? (1)

    12. In what form did God Appear? (2)

13. Why did Sarah laugh? (12)

14. When was the Lord to return and Sarah would have a son? (14)

15. In the verses we've read, how many times did the Lord promise Sarah would have a child by next year?

Genesis 21: 1-5

16. Did God fulfill the promises He made to Abraham? (1)

17. How old were Abraham and Sarah when Isaac was born? (5)

18. Was God on time – was He faithful to His word totally?

19. Can we rely on God to be faithful because of His track record?

Genesis 22:1-19

20. What did God ask Abraham to do? (2)

21. Does Abraham resolve to do what God asks? (3)

22. How many days did Abraham travel knowing that he will kill his son? (4)

23. Did Abraham believe that God would restore Isaac to him after Abraham killed him? (5)

24. How old do you think Isaac must have been to carry the wood on his back? (6)

25. Who was going to provide the lamb? (8)

26. How could Abraham have bound Isaac?

27. How do we know Abraham feared God? (12)

28. What was the substitute that God supplied for the sacrifice instead of Isaac? (13)

29. What did Abraham call the place where they were? (14)

30. This story was written down or copied by Moses approximately 500 years after it happened, what was the place still called? (14)

31. How was Abraham to be blessed for doing what God asked? (17,18)

32. How would all the nations be blessed by his offspring?

33. How did the writers of the Bible know which offspring of all the forefathers to follow in order to make the Bible be about Jesus?

Part 1 Questions Concerning Similar Events to Events in the New Testament

34. Was the birth of Isaac a miracle?
35. Was the birth of Christ a miracle?

36. Was Isaac's birth a fulfillment of a promise and prophecy?
37. Was Christ's birth a fulfillment of a promise and a prophecy?

38. Did God call Isaac, Abraham's one and only son whom you love?
39. Is Jesus called God's only son whom He loves?

40. Isaac was dead to Abraham (in his mind he knew he was going to kill him) as soon as he started on the journey – how long before Isaac was restored to his father?
41. How long was it before Jesus was restored to His Father after dying on the cross?

42. Did Isaac carry the wood for the sacrifice?
43. Did Jesus carry the wood for His sacrifice?

44. Did Isaac put up a fight when he was to be sacrificed?
45. Did Christ put up a fight when he was going to the cross?

46. What did God substitute for Isaac?
47. Why didn't he substitute a lamb as Abraham said he would?

48. Did that substitute have something around its head?
49. Did Christ have something around His head?

50. Abraham called the place he took Isaac – "The Lord will provide" and it's still called "On the mountain of the Lord it will be provided." Do you notice anything odd about the name?

Outline to Lesson- A Study on Abraham and Isaac

Part 2 Questions

Genesis 24:1-11

1. What did Abraham want his servant to do? (3,4)

2. If after the servant told a girl about Isaac she refused the offer, was Isaac going to go to the country himself to ask for a bride? (5,6)

3. Who did Abraham say that God would send before his servant? (7)

4. What if the bride still did not want to come? (8)

5. Did Rebekah agree to go?

6. When is the next time we hear about Isaac?

Open class Questions (No right or wrong answer)

7. What kind of feelings did you go through in reading this story?

8. What questions does this story answer about God's faithfulness and testing our faith?

Now Let's Look at Scripture:

> **"Abraham reasoned that God could raise the dead, and figuratively speaking, he did receive Isaac back from death."**
> **(NIV Heb, 11:19)**

> **"Accounting that God was able to raise him up, even from the dead; from whence also he received him in a figure."**
> **(KJV Heb. 11:19)**

This means that Abraham believed that God would raise Isaac from the dead and that idea was like the resurrection of Christ. Let's see if we can see more similar ideas.

Part two Questions Concerning Similar Events to Events in the New Testament

9. Did Abraham come down the mountain with Isaac?
10. After Christ ascended to heaven when will see Him next?

11. Did Abraham send someone to get Isaac a bride?
12. Does God the Father send someone to get a bride for Christ?

13. Did Abraham say that someone would go before his servant to prepare the Bride for the Servant's coming?
14. Does God send someone before the Holy Spirit to prepare the way?

15. Did the servant bring gifts to give people?
16. Does the Holy Spirit give gifts to people?

17. Who did the servant of Abraham talk about?
18. Who does the Holy Spirit reveal things about?

19. Who does the servant say is in charge of everything?
20. Who does the Bible/Holy Spirit reveal is in charge of everything?

21. If the girl would not come with Abraham's servant was he supposed to force her to come?
22. If people don't want to be Christians will God force them to be Christian anyway?

23. Did Eliezer Abraham's servant get a bride for Isaac?
24. Does the Holy Spirit bring the bride to Christ?

25. What was the end result of the servant getting the Bride?
26. What is the end result for the Holy Spirit bringing people to Christ?

27. What does Eliezer mean in Hebrew?
28. What did Jesus call the Holy Spirit?

Bible Study Abraham and Isaac (Teacher's copy)

Part 1 Questions

Genesis 12:7

1. What does God promise Abraham? (*God will give land to Abraham's offspring*)

2. Does this mean that Abraham will have at least one child from Sarah? (*Yes and probably a boy – inheritance usually went to the boys of the family Sarah was Abrahams wife God would not want Abraham to have another wife – the legitimate one would be the one God was talking about – she didn't die before Isaac was born – God would have known that*)

In Genesis 15: 1-6

3. Has a significant time passed between the above promise and this verse? (1-3) (*Yes because they remained childless*)

4. Who is the one Abram says will inherit his property? (2) (*Eliezer of Damascus*)

5. Does God repeat a similar promise as in chapter 12 above? (4,5) (*Yes it's even stronger*)

6. What was credited to Abram as righteousness? (6) (*His faith*)

7. How important was Abram's faith? How important is our faith today? (*Very important as it was counted as righteousness – for us Ephesians 2:8,9 we have been saved through faith and not works*)

Genesis 17:15-17

8. Why do you think that God changed Sarah's name? (15) (*Often times names change when God is going to use someone for his purpose although not always – note – Jacob to*)

Israel, Simon to Peter, Saul to Paul etc. it also signifies a new start or God changing someone's circumstances)

9. Why did Abraham laugh when God told him about a son? (17) (*Abraham was near 100 years old and Sarah was near 90 years old.*)

10. What was the child's name to be and when would Sarah have him? (19,21) (*Isaac by next year*)

Genesis 18:1…14

11. Did the Lord appear to Abraham? (1) (Yes)

12. In what form did God Appear? (2) (*A man's form – this is called a Theophany - appearance of Christ pre-incarnate*)

13. Why did Sarah laugh? (12) (*Because she was too old to have children*)

14. When was the Lord to return and Sarah would have a son? (10, 14) (*by next year*)

15. In the verses we've read, how many times did the Lord promise Sarah would have a child by next year? (*3*)

Genesis 21: 1-5

16. Did God fulfill the promises He made to Abraham? (1) (*Yes*)

17. How old were Abraham and Sarah when Isaac was born? (5) (*Approximately 100yrs. old and 90yrs. old - refer to earlier verses*).

18. Was God on time – was He faithful to His word totally? (*Yes*)

19. Can we rely on God to be faithful to us because of His track record? (*Yes*)

20. What did God ask Abraham to do? (2) (*Take your son your only son whom you love and sacrifice him on a mountain*)

21. Does Abraham resolve to do what God asks? (3) (*Yes and he does so immediately the next day*)

22. How many days did Abraham travel knowing that he will kill his son? (4) (*3 days*)

23. Did Abraham believe that God would restore Isaac to him after he killed him? (5) (*Yes*)

24. How old do you think Isaac must have been to carry the wood on his back? (6) (*Late teens to as late as 30s?*)

25. Who was going to provide the lamb? (8) (*God himself will provide the lamb*)

26. How could Abraham have bound Isaac? (*Isaac must have done it willingly without a struggle*)

27. How do we know Abraham feared God? (12) (*Because he did not withhold his son his only son*)

28. What was the substitute that God supplied for the sacrifice instead of Isaac? (*A ram*)

29. What did Abraham call the place where they were? (14) (*"The Lord will provide"*)

30. This story was written down or copied by Moses approximately 500 years after it happened, what was the place still called? (14) (*On the mountain of the Lord it will be provided*)

31. How was Abraham to be blessed for doing what God asked? (17,18) (*Making his descendant too numerous to count, taking cities of their enemies, and through his offspring nations will be blessed*)

32. How would all the nations be blessed by his offspring? (*because one of his offspring will be Jesus our Lord who blesses all nations*)

33. How did the writers of the Bible know which offspring of all the forefathers to follow in order to make the Bible be about Jesus? (*People often know who their ancestors are, but they cannot know their descendants hundreds of years before those descendants are born – that could only come from the inspiration of God. It's genealogy in reverse – He knows it backwards and forwards*)

Part 1 Questions Concerning Similar Events to Events in the New Testament

34. Was the birth of Isaac a miracle? (*Yes – Sarah was way too old to have children*)
35. Was the birth of Christ a miracle? (*Yes – Mary was a virgin*)

36. Was Isaac's birth a fulfillment of a promise and prophecy? (*yes*)
37. Was Christ's birth a fulfillment of a promise and a prophecy? (*yes*)

38. Did God call Isaac, Abraham's one and only son whom you love? (*Yes*)
39. Is Jesus called God's only son whom He loves? (*Yes*)

40. Isaac was dead to Abraham (in his mind he knew he was going to kill him) as soon as he started on the journey – how long before Isaac was restored to his father? (*3 days*)
41. How long was it before Jesus was restored to His Father after dying on the cross? (*3 days*)

42. Did Isaac carry the wood for the sacrifice? (*yes*)
43. Did Jesus carry the wood for His sacrifice? (*yes, his cross*)

44. Did Isaac put up a fight when he was to be sacrificed? (*no*)

45. Did Christ put up a fight when he was going to the cross? (*no*)

46. What did God substitute for Isaac? (*Ram*)
47. Why didn't he substitute a lamb as Abraham said he would? (*The lamb of God would come later in the form of Jesus Christ*)

48. Did that substitute have something around its head? (*Thorns – he was stuck by his horns*)
49. Did Christ have something around His head? (*yes a crown of thorns*)

50. Abraham called the place he took Isaac – "The Lord will provide" and it's still called "On the mountain of the Lord it will be provided." Do you notice anything odd about the name? (*Future tense even in Moses day and it was where Christ was crucified*)

Outline to Lesson- A Study on Abraham and Isaac (Teacher's Copy)

Part 2 Questions

Genesis 24:1-11

1. What did Abraham want his servant to do? (3,4) (*Get a Wife for his son*)

2. If after the servant told a girl about Isaac she refused the offer, was Isaac going to go to the country himself to ask for a bride? (5,6) (*No*)

3. Who did Abraham say that God would send before his servant? (7) (*An angel*)

4. What if the bride still did not want to come? (8) (*Then the servant is released from his oath*)

5. Did Rebekah agree to go? (*Odd that she was given the choice but she said yes and went*)

6. When is the next time we hear about Isaac? (*When Isaac sees his bride*)

Open class Questions (No right or wrong answer)

7. 7. What kind of feelings do you go through in reading this story. What questions does this story answer about God's faithfulness and testing our faith? (*A feeling of awesomeness that God keeps his promises to the letter, the idea of anguish that perhaps God would have felt when Jesus died on the cross, the caring that God has for man and the reward of faithfulness God gives us if we believe Him*)

8. What questions does this story answer about God's faithfulness and testing our faith?

Now Let's Look at Hebrews 11:19

> **"Abraham reasoned that God could raise the dead, and figuratively speaking, he did receive Isaac back from death."**
> **(NIV Heb. 11:19)**

> **"Accounting that God was able to raise him up, even from the dead; from whence also he received him in a figure."**
> **(KJV Heb. 11:19)**

This means that Abraham believed that God would raise Isaac from the dead and that idea was like the resurrection of Christ. Let's see if we can see more similarities.

Part 2 Questions Concerning Similar Events to Events in the New Testament

9. Did Abraham come down the mountain with Isaac? (*He is not talked about*)
10. After Christ ascended to heaven when will see Him next? (*When He comes for His bride*)

11. Did Abraham send someone to get Isaac a bride? (*Yes*)
12. Does God the Father send someone to get a bride for Christ? (*Yes – first of all Christians, those who love Jesus Christ are called His Bride and we're told that God sends the Holy Spirit to convict and comfort us as believers and bring us to Christ.*)

13. Did Abraham say that someone would go before his servant to prepare the Bride for the Servant's coming? (*Yes- God would send an angel*)
14. Does God send someone before the Holy Spirit to prepare the way? (*Yes – us*)

15. Did the servant bring gifts to give people? (*Yes*)
16. Does the Holy Spirit give gifts to people? (*Yes*)

17. Who did the servant of Abraham talk about? (*His son Isaac*)
18. Who does the Holy Spirit reveal things about? (*God's Son Jesus*)

19. Who does the servant say is in charge of everything of His father Abraham? (*his son Isaac*)
20. Who does the Bible/Holy Spirit reveal is in charge of everything of His father in heaven? (*Jesus His Son*)

21. If the girl would not come with Abraham's servant was he to force her to come? (*No*)
22. If people don't want to be Christians will God force them to be? (*No*)

23. Did Eliezer Abraham's servant get a bride for Isaac? (*yes*)
24. Does the Holy Spirit bring the bride to Christ? (*yes*)

25. What was the end result of the servant getting the Bride? (*Uniting with the Isaac and a wedding*)
26. What is the end result for the Holy Spirit bringing people to Christ? (*Uniting with Christ and a wedding*)

27. What does Eliezer mean in Hebrew? (*God of help or God is help – some say God the comforter*)
28. What did Jesus call the Holy Spirit? (*The comforter*)

A few other things to recap:

The servant we learned earlier in Genesis was named Eliezer and he was told by Abraham to get a bride for Isaac – Eliezer told the bride how wealthy Isaac was and that how everything Abraham had was now is Isaacs. He speaking about Isaac all the time. And when Rebekah decided to be betrothed to Isaac the servant, Eliezer, gave her gifts and brought her to Isaac – Isaac was not to go back to the land where Rebekah lived to get a bride if the bride doesn't come.

First of all, the Holy Spirit is called the "Comforter" by Christ. Eliezer means comforter. The Holy Spirit Tells us of the things of Christ and the Bible tells us that God the Father has put everything under His control. He has everything of the Father's. The Holy Spirit gives gifts to everyone that accepts Christ as the Lord and Savior. Christ of course is called the bridegroom – we are the bride and we become betrothed to Christ. The

Holy Spirit leads us to Christ. After Christ's crucifixion He will not to be seen again until it's to meet His bride in the air. He will never come back to earth again to get people to become His bride. We must come to Him by what the Holy Spirit and the Bible tells us and nothing else.

Encouraging Bible Study Stories

I have, throughout my time as a Bible studies leader, encountered inspiring events and individuals who helped me along my path as a teacher. You will encounter your own events as you follow your own path. It's important from time to time to remember and look back on people that you have affected as well as people who affected you.

Every time we give out the Word of God, it never comes back void. Yesterday I went to church and one of the men in the stories I've included came up to me and said that his church's pastor asked everyone to tell about the person that effected them the most in their Christian walk. He said I told them about you. I relate this story to you not in a bragging matter, but more in humility. It's God and God alone who affects people. He uses people to deliver His message.

God knows who needs to be encouraged and when. Yesterday was my turn and I greatly appreciated knowing how this man felt. To think that he would mention me under those circumstances meant the world to me. God was allowing me to be blessed by his comments and how he felt. I know full well that God is the One who makes me look good to others. Without His promptings and His urgings, nothing could ever be accomplished.

Lima NY group

One of my all-time favorite Bible Study Group stories was about how my group from Lima, New York got started. Lima is about 20 miles outside of Rochester, New York where I live. The study lasted for approximately 5 years.

My friend Bob was at a family's home in Lima and had been trying to open the door to have me come over and talk with them about the Lord for a few months. Bob knew these people for some 30 years. As close friends, he was very concerned about their salvation and he wanted to know that they would be in Heaven with him. So once again, he was witnessing to them.

One day, I received a call that from Bob, who immediately said, "Hey, what are you doing?" I said that I was working, why? He said, "I need you to get over here as soon as you can to talk with three of my friends." The three people were Cappy, his wife Carol, and their friend John. I told Bob that we would have to wait until the next day, as I had to get Bibles for all three. So he made the date.

The following day I arrived at Cappy and Carol's home to find Bob and the other three seated around the kitchen table. I gave Cappy and Carol their Bibles but when I started to give the Bible to John he just pushed it back across the table at me and said "That's ok I'm just going to listen, I'm a skeptic". I said "no problem."

We started on the first of four lessons that I give for beginning Bible studies and people I witness to. Everyone was cordial and didn't have a lot of questions. After the first lesson was over we made a date for me to come back, but I wasn't really sure whether John would come back or not.

When the next day to study came, I was back out in Lima and John was there. He really was a very nice guy but had some bad experiences in another church when he was younger. So there were reasons for his skepticism. As I sat down at the table questions started to flow. They must have gotten together between the first day I was there and the second day as they were reminding each other of questions that they had. Although we didn't get to our second study of the four, we had just a great time talking about their questions and opening the Bible to find answers for them.

It was a wonderful six weeks of study. What usually takes four weeks took two extra weeks because of the conversations and questions surrounding the Bible. That kind of passion for understanding the Bible and the thoughtful questions raised, encouraged and added an air of excitement that was second to none for me. I look back on that time with thankfulness to God for the privilege of being allowed to witness to these three people. I should mention that the average age was well over retirement.

All three became baptized believers after that six-week period. They loved it so much that we continued meeting for the next five years. They all became members of my home church.

Some sidelights were:

Four other people became believers from that study at Cappy's house.

I was privileged to be at Cappy's home and pray with him the night he died. The doctors let him come home from the hospital and he had a wonderful meal. We talked about the Lord and then he fell asleep in the chair. As the night went on, we could not wake Cappy up. He was in a comatose like state except we knew he could still hear and his face looked anxious. So, I prayed for him a very personal private prayer and his face started looking peaceful once again. He died 6 hours later. It was his time and the Lord was so gracious to allow me into that intimate moment.

As for John, it was a complete turn-around. I started a Bible study at John's home with two other people. He also brought me to his son and daughter-in-law's house, we watched the Lord draw them in, and they became believers. After that, John took me to his niece's house, his ex-partner's house, and one other friend. All but his ex-partner came to the Lord.

Three months after John became a believer, on a visit to his home, he met me outside. There he said, "Brent, I have never seen such a great day as this. Look at what the Lord has made". From a skeptic to a believer – firm and staunch. Only the Lord can do that.

John died one year after Cappy, and Carol one year after that. They are at home with the Lord. Thanks be to God!

Carol

The first time I met Carol was at a long time Bible study with two of my friends I met from work. One day she came, and at the time, as it is with all of these memories, I didn't know what an impact we would have on each other. She listened to what we were talking about and asked some questions. I asked if she would like to come back the following week and we would start on the four initial lessens again. She said she would. After we finished the four lessons, Carol became a baptized believer.

Shortly after that, Carol asked me to start a Bible study in her home in Victor, New York (About 40 minutes from my home). I of course said yes. I try to involve other Christians in my Bible studies wherever possible. In this case, because we were starting a new Bible study group and the main student starting it was a woman, I ALWAYS brought someone with me. Most of the time, I brought a retired man by the name of Harry with me to Carol's house. But, if Harry couldn't make it, I brought another Christian brother with me.

Carol became a member of my church and for the rest of her life would drive 40 minutes every Sunday to come to church. We tried to get her involved with churches in her neighborhood so she wouldn't have to drive so far, but she insisted that our church was the only church she wanted to go to.

During the Bible study at Carol's house God led five people to Christ and several others to study with us that were already Christians. Carol told me some years later that at the time we first met she was contemplating suicide. That shocked me because she was so outgoing and personable. But, God knows what He is doing and Carol became an avid believer affecting everyone she came in contact with. She would go to be with her savior over 12 years after coming to Him.

When Carol first became sick and things weren't going well, a doctor asked her how she could be so upbeat. Her answer was "I believe in Jesus and that's how He would want me to be. I have to go through this faithfully so others can see what Jesus means to me – maybe they will want to come to Him too." Of course she witnessed to the doctors whenever she could.

From thoughts of a suicide to a wonderful Christian willing to go through any hardship, "The way Jesus would want," is such a drastic turnaround. What a wonderful God we have and what a privilege Bible study teachers are given to be used by God for His eternal purposes.

Abby and Jennifer

As I worked for over 40 years in the home improvement industry, I was constantly coming in contact with people in their homes while doing work for them. I had done work for Abby and her family for ten or twelve years before coming to the Lord. Sometime after that, I was again involved in another project for them.

As usual, I would stop over and check on the men every couple of days. On one particular day, we were working on a mudroom right next to the kitchen and Abby offered us coffee. She also wanted to go over a part of the project with me and as we were talking, she changed the subject to say that she was excited because she and Jennifer were going to a seminar on Wicca. Wicca is, of course, the name associated with witchcraft.

This opened the door that I always look for to witness to people.

I learned early on in witnessing, it is much better to take the approach of sharing ideas, rather than just immediately dismissing ideas that are not Biblical (which is my natural tendency). So I just asked her to let me know what she and Jennifer found out.

A couple of days later when I stopped to check the progress on the renovation, Abby was excited to tell me all about her experience. I asked her if she ever studied the Bible or went to church. She said she had, but it wasn't very fulfilling. I asked if she had a Bible and could I show her something that might have a bearing on exactly what she was talking about. That started a Bible study with Abby and Jennifer.

I think of all the Bible studies I have ever done, Abby had the most questions and the most thought provoking ideas, bar none. Sometimes this type of person can be very distracting from a Bible study, but it was a great proving ground for me as a young teacher to have. The Lord knows how to school us and put people in our path at just the right time to enable us to become more prepared and useful for His glory.

After coming to the Lord, Abby and Jennifer came to the women's study at Bob's house every week and became members of my home church. If there was a baptism she was there to cheer new believers on.

When People say that they are going to a seminar or anything like that, it means they are searching. It is up to all of us as believers to do whatever we can to show people the Word of God. God will teach people what they need to know. If we don't get out God's Word, people will fill the void with very poor substitutes that could mean the eternal condemnation.

It is a truly awesome sight to see a person who has a thirst for filling a void in their heart come to God. What a difference and thrill it is to see

God's hand at work in these people's quest for the truth. What a life-changing event when a wonderful new birth takes place.

Tim

Tim was a postman and I was on his mail route. Years before coming to the Lord, Tim had given me a couple of projects to do on his home. The subject of the Lord never came up because we were both in the same place in terms of having little to no faith in anything.

Some years later, he called me for another project. His dad had passed away and his mom was coming to live with him. They wanted to talk about remodeling the upstairs to make a nice place for his mom to live in.

When I stopped over to talk to him his mother was there. She loved the Lord and asked me whether I did also. What a wonderful opening for talking about my favorite subject. I came to the Lord two years before, and I was interested in talking with anyone or anybody about my love for Jesus. As God always works things out, I found out they attended the same church at the same time as my mother and father did, when I was young. It was kind of like old home week. But, Tim was not interested in our discussion, and was no longer attending any church.

Tim and I had a lot in common. He was one month younger than I was and we had similar experiences growing up. However, as far as the Lord was concerned, it seemed that I had more in common with his mother than I had with Tim.

Shortly after that visit, I received a call from Tim asking me to come over again, this time for supper, as his mother was coming back to town. Under the guise of wanting to hear more about the renovation of her new rooms, she really wanted me to talk to Tim about the Lord.

When I came for dinner, I brought my Bible and as carefully as possible, I brought up the talk we had the previous time I visited. We ended up having a Bible study after dinner. As usual, we started on the initial Bible study. Tim seemed a little more interested than before and agreed, with his mother's coaxing, to have me come back next week for another lesson.

To make a long story short Tim came to the Lord and started coming to church with me. He has become a staunch Christian and is still with me for Bible studies, both on Tuesdays and at church on Sunday morning. We have become very good friends over the years and are as close as brothers can be.

He later told me that he felt that if we hadn't had those Bible studies he never would have gotten out of the bad life style he was living. Isn't God wonderful – What a wonderful God we have!

Ron

I met Ron for the first time at a friend's house. A little while later he wanted me to stop and talk about an improvement he wanted to make on his home.

Ron is a very personable guy and when I went to his house, I felt at home right away. After a few minutes of conversation, I brought up the idea of going to church because he lived close to the church I was going to. He explained that he had come to the Lord some years back but had drifted away because he felt mad at God.

As we talked, I realized that Ron was a very passionate but logical person. He couldn't understand why God would let his father be taken from him at such an early age. He had thought through his anger at God and he felt justified to have the resentment he felt toward God. I knew that he needed to hear God's word in a little different way. I reasoned of course that it was God's territory to draw Ron into His word.

I asked him if he had a Bible – he did, so I gave him part of the initial lesson on the Bible. After a few weeks of talking and showing him things in the Bible, I think God softened his heart and he came to church. He also started coming to my Thursday Bible study.

Since then, Ron and I have appeared in several plays and he currently attends a Tuesday night men's Bible study. He also goes on mission trips regularly. For a while, he was a ministry leader heading up missions.

A confirmed Christian and worker for the Lord, Ron is now come back to his first love – Jesus his Savior. All brought about by a Bible study and subsequent involvement with other Christians.

Ron was also a presider for our church. Before we take communion or the offering men of the church stand up and give a short meditation to give people the opportunity to focus on what is happening. Ron is one of those people called presiders. I look forward to hearing when it's his turn to speak. He has an insight and manner of speaking with confidence and heart that is just wonderful to listen to.

He is also my Christian brother and a very close friend. He is one of the people I look for in a crowd.

God wants us to be his helper in getting the message out and he doesn't let His word return void of power. It is through us, His own, that God works his wonderful Teachings. What a tremendous experience we can have if we only open up to our Father in Heaven to be used by Him.

Bill

Bill was a son-in-law of a friend of mine. He was also an alcoholic and he would on occasion hit his wife.

One day, I got a call from my friend asking me to go with him to his daughter's house as Bill was at it again and he wanted me to stop him from killing Bill. I went with him.

When we got there he was just being taken away by ambulance as he was hurt trying to break into his car to get at his wife and children. My friend immediately took the family to his house and forbid Bill ever to come there and see them.

This arrangement worked out all right for a few weeks, but then his daughter asked her father if Bill could come and stay there with her. The original request was turned down flat.

But, the tension and problems with this were mounting. So an arrangement was made that Bill could come back IF he would agree to go take my beginners class for four weeks. After some moaning and groaning, Bill agreed to take the classes and we met at my house.

The first time Bill came to class you could tell he was really mad about being there. He kept his hands folded in front of him the entire time. We tried to make him feel welcome and comfortable as I went through the first class with him. He reluctantly agreed to come the following week. It seemed he was coming only because of the situation and he was not happy about it.

When it got close to the appointment for the next week, I was really unsure if he would make it. But, I was surprised that he actually showed up. I believe that it was the idea that he couldn't be with his children and his wife if he didn't continue that made the difference. But, there was something in his eyes, a demeanor that had changed. He was listening intently to what I was saying. There was a true change coming from his heart. God has a way of working miracles in people's lives and I was about to see one.

By the third week, he seemed like an avid Bible student who really wanted to learn. He was as animated as I had ever seen him. Asking questions and getting thoroughly involved with the answers. No longer were his arms folded but he was using them to talk and put emphasis on the points he was asking about.

The fourth week (4th and final lesson) he was so excited that he wanted to be baptized the following Sunday.

What a change in four weeks. God is a God of miracles and love. Touching Bill in a way only He could. Bill was very enthusiastic and happy.

When Sunday came, I had the privilege of lowering Bill into the water for his baptism. When he came out of the water, his face shone and he was beaming. Something happened to Bill in the previous four weeks. That Sunday he let it all out. He had a God given joy that anyone could see. It seemed for the first time he could smile and truly look at life differently.

He has never beaten his wife again as far as I know. He doesn't drink and he's been working steadily at his job ever since. This transformation by God was one of the most miraculous that I have personally witnessed. You may hear of these things happening but you won't truly believe it until it happens right in front of you. That is exactly what happened to me. Bill, completely transformed, was given the strength to make it for about twenty more years.

Thank you, Lord, for the wonderful transformation in Bill's life.

Bible Verse List

Bibliography

Goodrick, Edward W., and John R. Kohlenberger. *The Strongest NIV Exhaustive Concordance.* Zondervan, 1999.

The Holy Bible, New International Version. International Bible Society, 1984.

The King James Version of the Bible. Thomas Nelson Incorporated, 1988.

McGee, J. Vernon. *Thru the Bible Series.* T. Nelson, 1981.

Serendipity Bible for Groups. Serendipity Group, 1988.

Strong, James. *The New Strong's Exhaustive Concordance of the Bible.* Thomas Nelson Publishers, 1990.

World Bible Translation Center, Inc. "Matthew Henry Commentary on the Whole Bible." *Holy Bible: Easy-to-Read Version,* e-Sword- the Sword of the LORD with an electronic edge, 2008, Accessed 2022.

World Bible Translation Center, Inc. "Albert Barnes' Notes on the Bible." *Holy Bible: Easy-to-Read Version,* e-Sword- the Sword of the LORD with an electronic edge, 2008, Accessed 2022.

World Bible Translation Center, Inc. "John Gill's Exposition of the Bible." *Holy Bible: Easy-to-Read Version,* e-Sword- the Sword of the LORD with an electronic edge, 2008, Accessed 2022.

World Bible Translation Center, Inc. "Jamieson-Fausset-Brown Commentary." *Holy Bible: Easy-to-Read Version,* e-Sword- the Sword of the LORD with an electronic edge, 2008, Accessed 2022.

World Bible Translation Center, Inc. "Adam Clarke's Commentary on the Bible." *Holy Bible: Easy-to-Read Version,* e-Sword- the Sword of the LORD with an electronic edge, 2008, Accessed 2022.